BBC

DOCTOR WHO

CHARACTER ENCYCLOPEDIA

BBC

DOCTOR WHO

CHARACTER ENCYCLOPEDIA

WRITTEN BY

JASON LOBORIK, ANNABEL GIBSON & MORAY LAING

CONTENTS

Who created the Daleks? Which alien is able to create a black hole wherever it wants? Who has accompanied the Doctor on his space and time travels in the TARDIS? The Time Lord has met many aliens, cyborgs, robots and humans on his journeys through history and across the universe. Some have tried to EX-TER-MIN-ATE him, while others have formed lasting friendships with him...

FINDING A CHARACTER

Look up characters alphabetically by their first name or title, or use the index on pages 204–207. Below is a list of all the characters categorised by type, listed beneath the colour that features at the top of the character's page entry.

ALIEN

COMPANION

CYBORG

EARTH CREATURE

ENTITY

HUMAN

ROBOT

TIME LORD

ABZORBALOFF

GREEDY SHAPE-SHIFTING HUMANOID

The Abzorbaloff is a vile green alien from Clom, the twin planet of Raxacoricofallapatorius. The creature can absorb people into his body simply by touching them – feasting on their life force and experiences in the process. He is determined to find the Doctor, believing the Time Lord would be the greatest feast of all.

A STICKY END
The Abzorbaloff disguises himself as a human called Victor Kennedy and takes charge of LINDA, a motley band of people searching for the Doctor. The Abzorbaloff plans to use the TARDIS to return home in triumph.

DATA FILE

HOMEWORLD:
CLOM

SPECIAL ABILITIES:
ABSORBING OTHER LIFE FORMS, DISGUISING HIS APPEARANCE

DOCTORS MET:
10TH

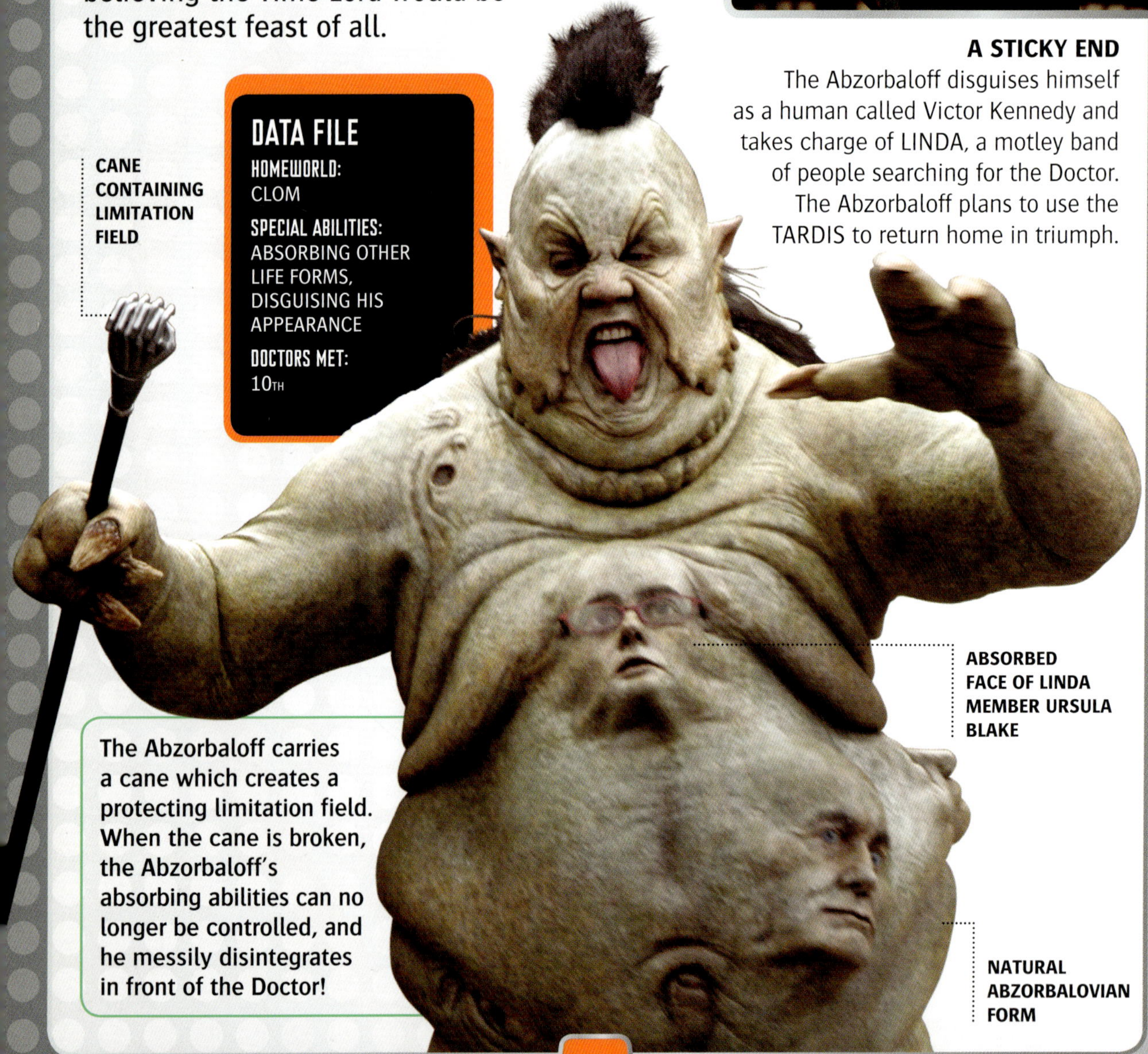

The Abzorbaloff carries a cane which creates a protecting limitation field. When the cane is broken, the Abzorbaloff's absorbing abilities can no longer be controlled, and he messily disintegrates in front of the Doctor!

ACE
TEARAWAY COMPANION

Ace is a tough, streetwise teenager who is transported in a time storm to Iceworld where she meets the Seventh Doctor. Embarrassed by her real name Dorothy, she assumes the nickname Ace. She becomes a close companion of the Doctor, whom she calls “Professor”, even though he disapproves of her tendency to blow things up with Nitro 9 – her homemade brand of explosives.

BASHING DALEKS

One Dalek becomes the unlucky recipient of Ace’s violent streak. Determined to defend herself, Ace bashes it to bits with a baseball bat powered by the Hand of Omega, knocking off its eye stalk in the process!

DATA FILE

ORIGIN:
PERIVALE, LONDON

OCCUPATION:
WAITRESS (SACKED)

DOCTORS MET:
7TH

Due to a rocky relationship with her mother, Ace had a difficult childhood and became something of a tearaway. Realising this, the Doctor encourages her to confront her fears, helping her to mature into a wiser and happier person.

ADAM MITCHELL
SHORT-TERM COMPANION

Adam is a young, day-dreaming genius who works for Henry Van Statten, a billionaire and collector of alien artefacts. Adam's job is to catalogue each strange object and work out its purpose. After surviving a lone Dalek's killing spree, he briefly joins the Ninth Doctor on his travels.

Adam steals secrets from the future and plans to profit from them when he returns to the 21st century. The Doctor is furious when he finds out and immediately takes Adam back home, warning him to keep his infospike a secret.

HOLE IN THE HEAD
In the year 200,000, Adam has surgery aboard the Satellite Five space station to install an infospike, an advanced computer interface port, into his forehead. When he clicks his fingers, the centre of the device opens up, exposing his brain and allowing it to receive vast amounts of advanced information.

ALIEN ARTEFACTS
Before meeting the Doctor, Adam studies alien artefacts in a bunker belonging to Henry Van Statten.

DATA FILE

ORIGIN:
ENGLAND, EARTH

OCCUPATION:
GENIUS, SCIENTIFIC RESEARCHER

DOCTORS MET:
9TH

ADELAIDE BROOKE
COMMANDER OF BOWIE BASE ONE

Captain Adelaide Brooke is the leader of the first human colony on Mars. She tells the Doctor that as a ten-year-old girl, she saw a Dalek appear at her window, then fly away. She knew one day she would follow it into space.

HAIR WORN OFF FACE

GREEN COMBAT UNIFORM

WATERTIGHT BOOTS

DATA FILE
ORIGIN: FINCHLEY, NORTH LONDON, EARTH
OCCUPATION: COMMANDER
DOCTORS MET: 10TH

Adelaide is a tough, intelligent and single-minded authority figure. However, she cares deeply about her crew and is devastated when she realises she will be unable to save them.

FLOOD ALERT
In November 2059, Adelaide is plunged into a terrifying crisis when infected water starts leaking through the roof – turning her crew into zombies called the Flood.

A FIXED POINT IN HISTORY?
Adelaide's death would inspire her descendents to travel into space, but the Doctor decides to change history and save her life. When Adelaide realises this, she tells him he was wrong and takes her own life.

ADIPOSE
LIVING FAT MONSTERS

The Adipose are cute, friendly aliens made of human fat. When dieting, humans take a pill made by Adipose Industries. Baby Adipose then grow inside their bodies before bursting out of their skin, taking their hosts' excess fat with them. To the world, it seems like the ultimate cure for obesity!

The Doctor learns that the Adipose are being bred illegally by Matron Cofelia, an intergalactic super-nanny who is working for the Adiposian First Family. Eventually, a huge spaceship appears to take the cute creatures back to the stars.

MATRON COFELIA
Calm, arrogant Matron Cofelia goes to Earth undercover as "Miss Foster" trying to find obesity. She needs to breed a new generation after the Adipose nursery planet was lost.

MONSTERS ON THE MOVE
One night, many thousands of baby Adipose leave their host bodies and begin marching through the streets of London, much to the astonishment of passers-by.

DATA FILE
ORIGIN:
ADIPOSE 3
SPECIAL ABILITIES:
CAN CONVERT MOST HUMAN TISSUE INTO ADIPOSE
DOCTORS MET:
10TH

ADRIC
GENIUS COMPANION

Adric is a teenage genius from the planet Alzarius, whose own people once gave him a badge for mathematical excellence. When his brother Varsh is killed by Marshmen, Adric stows aboard the TARDIS, although he sometimes finds it hard getting on with his fellow travellers and often feels like an outsider.

DATA FILE

HOMEWORLD:
ALZARIUS, E-SPACE

OCCUPATION:
UNKNOWN

DOCTORS MET:
4TH, 5TH

LAYING TRAPS
Following the Fourth Doctor's regeneration, Adric is kidnapped by the Master. He uses the boy's mathematical skills to create a space-time trap for the Doctor – the bizarre city of Castrovalva.

After fighting the Terileptils, Urbankans and the Mara, Adric's final battle is against the Cybermen. He tries to stop them crashing a spaceship into Earth but sadly dies in the attempt, never to know that the explosion was responsible for wiping out the dinosaurs.

AGGEDOR
ROYAL BEAST OF PELADON

Originally found roaming around on the troubled planet of Peladon, the powerful, furry Aggedor creatures were hunted by the Pel people to the point of extinction. Considered as the Royal Beast of Peladon, legends refer to Aggedor one day returning and the great danger that will follow as a result.

ROYAL EMBLEM
Imagery of Aggedor appears throughout the Citadel of Peladon. Aggedor's head is also the royal emblem and its fur is used on royal clothing.

The Pels worship the spirit of Aggedor and are unaware that one of the creatures lives on in the caves of Peladon. It is used to scare off the Galactic Federation.

DATA FILE

HOMEWORLD:
PELADON

SPECIAL ABILITIES:
STRENGTH, ABLE TO SCARE

DOCTORS MET:
3RD

THE ALLIANCE

MASSIVE MONSTER ARMY

The Alliance is a confederation of the Doctor's deadliest enemies. Normally bitter foes, these monsters unite in their desire to stop the Doctor from destroying the universe. Millions of them gather in spaceships above Stonehenge when a prison box called the Pandorica opens to trap the Doctor inside.

The Alliance includes Daleks, Cybermen, Autons, Uvodni, Roboforms, Terileptils, Slitheen, Chelonians, Nestene, Drahvins, Sycorax, Haemogoths, Zygons, Atraxi, Draconians, Silurians, Sontarans, Judoon, Hoix and many others!

DATA FILE

HOMEWORLD:
VARIOUS

SPECIAL ABILITIES:
MASSIVE COMBINED POWER

DOCTORS MET:
11TH

DEADLY FOSSILS

The Alliance's trap doesn't stop the TARDIS exploding. A Total Event Collapse deletes almost everything from existence. Two stone Daleks survive and attack the Doctor in the National Museum in 1996.

ALPHA CENTAURI
SIX-ARMED ALIENS

Instantly recognisable by their one huge, bulbous eye, these creatures have a distinctive high-pitched voice, green skin and six arms. They are a nervous race, which shows in their uneasy demeanour. One of them is an alien delegate working on behalf of the Galactic Federation.

ALIEN DELEGATES
Alpha Centauri is just one of the alien delegates sent to Peladon. Other delegates include Ice Warriors, Arcturus and two delegates from Earth (who are actually the Doctor and his companion Jo Grant).

The Doctor calls Alpha Centauri a "hermaphrodite hexapod" – it is neither male nor female. The poor creature appears to be quite timid and shrieks with panic when scared. And when Sarah Jane Smith meets Alpha Centauri, the strong, young journalist is frustrated by its treatment of women – it considers females to be unimportant.

DATA FILE

HOMEWORLD:
ALPHA CENTAURI

CHARACTER TRAITS:
FRIGHTENING HUMANS (UNINTENTIONALLY)

DOCTORS MET:
3RD

AMY POND
GUTSY COMPANION

Amy's real name is Amelia. Witty, feisty and just a little stubborn, Amy had a difficult childhood, and was raised by her Aunt Sharon after a space-time crack in her bedroom wall swallowed up both her parents. She eventually marries her childhood friend, Rory Williams, and they travel together with the Doctor.

DATA FILE

ORIGIN:
SCOTLAND, EARTH

OCCUPATION:
FORMER KISSOGRAM AND MODEL, TRAVEL WRITER

DOCTOR MET:
11TH

LEATHER JACKET SHOWS HER TOUGH SIDE

RAGGEDY FRIEND

Amy first meets the Eleventh Doctor when he crash-lands the TARDIS in her back garden and fixes the space-time crack in her bedroom wall. Dazzled by her "Raggedy Doctor", she has to wait 14 years before getting a chance to travel with him, but when she does they become close friends.

RIVER'S REVELATION

During the Battle of Demon's Run, a distraught Amy loses her daughter Melody to The Silence. However, she's even more shocked when River Song announces that she is Melody, all grown up!

When a Weeping Angel zaps Rory back in time, Amy makes the emotional decision to let the angel send her back as well, meaning she won't ever see the Doctor again. She ends up living out her life with Rory, her beloved husband.

STURDY BOOTS PERFECT FOR ANY ADVENTURE

ASTRID PETH
BRAVE *TITANIC* WAITRESS

Astrid Peth, citizen of Sto, becomes a waitress on the *Titanic* spaceship to see the universe. When starliner owner Max Capricorn sabotages his own ship, Astrid teams up with the Doctor to fight Max's Heavenly Host robots and stop the *Titanic* from crashing into Earth.

DATA FILE

HOMEWORLD:
STO

SPECIAL ABILITIES:
QUICK THINKING AND BRAVERY

DOCTORS MET:
10TH

Astrid spends three years working at a spaceport diner before joining the crew of the *Titanic*. She dreams of travelling to other worlds, but it isn't until the Doctor sneaks her onto Earth that she stands on a different planet.

RELEASED TO THE STARS
Astrid is wearing a teleport bracelet when she falls. The Doctor tries to save her body but the system is too badly damaged. All that is left is an echo of her consciousness, which he releases to fly amongst the stars.

FALLING FAST
On learning of Max Capricorn's plans to destroy Earth, Astrid drives a fork-lift truck into his life-support machine, plunging them both into the Nuclear Storm Drive.

ATRAXI
ALIEN POLICE FORCE

The Atraxi are large crystalline-shaped wardens in charge of an extra-dimensional prison. They come to Earth in search of Prisoner Zero, a shape-changing alien who has escaped through a crack in time. The Atraxi send out a short but terrifying message, warning humanity that the entire planet will be incinerated unless Prisoner Zero is returned to them.

DATA FILE

ORIGIN:
UNKNOWN

SPECIAL ABILITIES:
REMOTE CONTROL OF ELECTRONIC DEVICES

DOCTORS MET:
11TH

CRYSTALLINE STRUCTURE RESEMBLES SNOWFLAKE

EXTENDABLE SINGLE EYE

THE DOCTOR'S WARNING

After tracking down Prisoner Zero himself, the newly regenerated Doctor summons the Atraxi and tells them to leave Earth alone in the future, warning them that the planet is well defended.

The Atraxi possess advanced technology. They manage to seal off Earth's atmosphere with a force field and are also able to take control of TVs and radios across the world, using them to broadcast their scary message in multiple languages.

AUTONS

KILLER SHOP DUMMIES

The Autons are the blank-faced servants of the Nestene Consciousness, a disembodied alien entity that has made several attempts to conquer Earth. The Consciousness has the ability to bring any form of plastic to life and uses its murderous mannequins to clear the way for invasion.

PLASTIC BODIES AND FACES

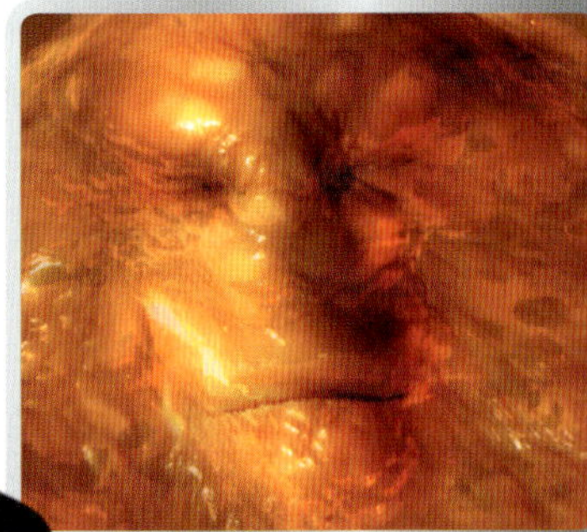

NESTENE
The Nestene Consciousness's real body is originally multi-tentacled. However, after the stresses of a war, it becomes liquid with a humanoid face.

DATA FILE

HOMEWORLD:
UNKNOWN

SPECIAL FEATURES:
HIDDEN WEAPONRY IN THEIR HANDS

DOCTORS MET:
3rd, 9th, 11th

SMART SUITS FROM HIGH STREET STORE

DUMMIES ON THE LOOSE
As part of the Nestene plan to turn Earth into a source of food, hordes of Autons burst from shop windows all over the world and gun down innocent passers-by!

While most Autons are crude-looking dummies, some are plastic copies of living people who look and sound like the real thing. In order to maintain a copy, the Nestene Consciousness needs to keep the original human alive.

AXONS
PARASITE RACE

This race of beautiful, gold-skinned humanoids first appears to be made up of four kind aliens with genuinely peaceful intentions. Their large organic ship contains an adult male and female with two child Axons. They tell Earth that their homeworld has been destroyed.

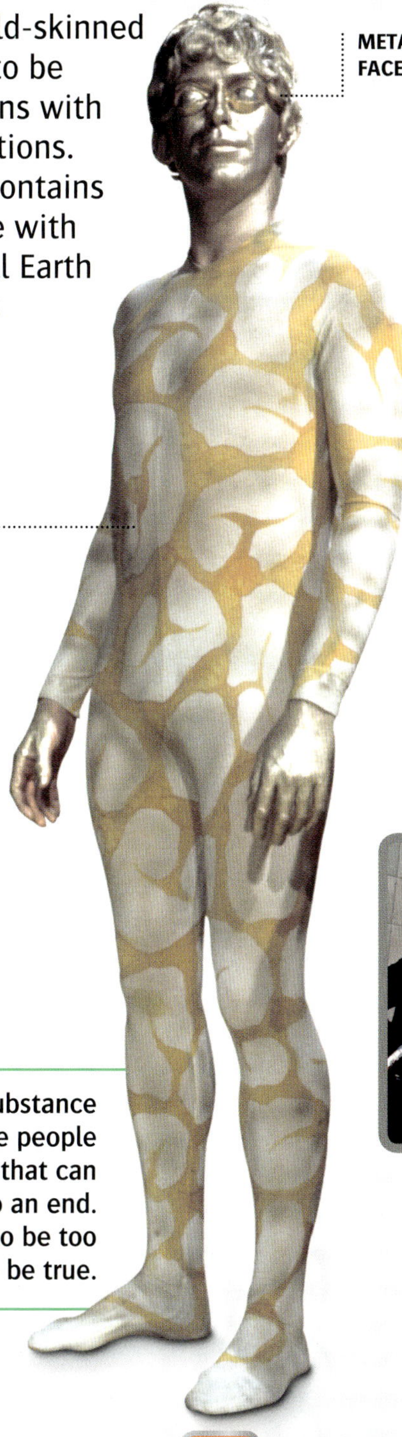

AXON SECRET
The gold-humanoid aliens are hideous, red-tentacled monsters in disguise. "Axonite" and the monsters are actually one giant creature called "Axos". The parasitic race is after just one thing – the energy of Earth.

DATA FILE
HOMEWORLD:
AXOS
SPECIAL ABILITIES:
SHAPE-CHANGING, ENERGY ABSORBING
DOCTORS MET:
3RD

The Axons offer a substance called Axonite to the people of Earth – a material that can bring world famine to an end. The gift proves to be too good to be true.

MASTER PLANS
The Axon creatures capture the Doctor's old enemy, the Master, as well as his TARDIS. The renegade Time Lord brings them to Earth so they can feed from the planet and drain its energy.

AZAL

LAST OF THE DÆMONS

Azal is the last of the powerful Dæmons from the planet Dæmos. He arrived on Earth thousands of years ago, influencing humanity's development as part of a great experiment performed by his race. Azal's image is familiar to humans, and he is partly responsible for humans' idea of the Devil.

DATA FILE

HOMEWORLD:
DÆMOS

SPECIAL ABILITIES:
CAN CHANGE SIZE RAPIDLY AND CREATE HEAT BARRIERS

DOCTORS MET:
3RD

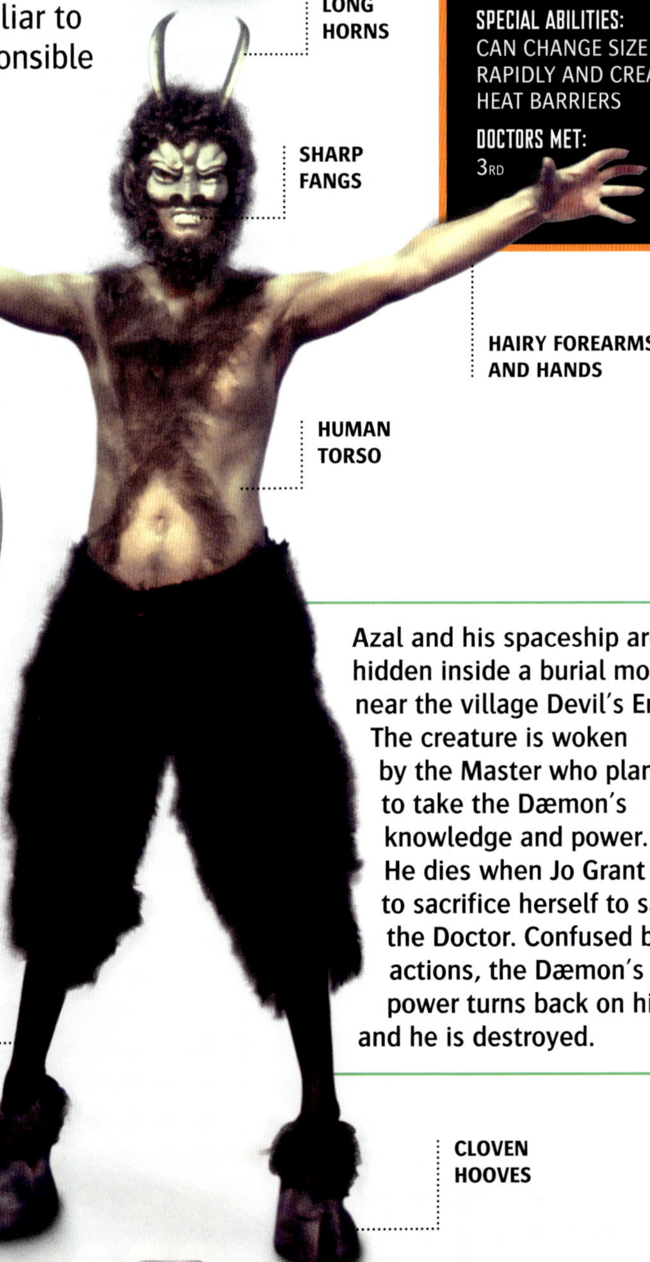

Azal and his spaceship are hidden inside a burial mound near the village Devil's End. The creature is woken by the Master who plans to take the Dæmon's knowledge and power. He dies when Jo Grant tries to sacrifice herself to save the Doctor. Confused by Jo's actions, the Dæmon's power turns back on himself and he is destroyed.

STONEY FACE

Bok is a stone gargoyle brought to life by Azal's power. Bok helps the Master at Devil's End and when Azal dies, the gargoyle returns to stone.

BANNAKAFFALATTA
ZOCCI *TITANIC* PASSENGER

Bannakaffalatta is a Zocci who travels on the *Titanic* spaceship. The Doctor says he looks like a "talking conker" and worries that he may start a riot when they teleport to Earth. Bannakaffalatta is actually a cyborg, the result of an accident years earlier on the planet Sto.

CYBORG SECRET
Bannakaffalatta only admits to *Titanic* waitress Astrid Peth that he is a cyborg because he has a crush on her. He makes her promise to keep his secret, then asks her to marry him!

Spiky by shape and by nature, Bannakaffalatta doesn't like his name being shortened to Banna. But while he is small and grumpy, he is also very brave.

FATAL BLAST
Bannakaffalatta is embarrassed to be a cyborg, but the EMP device implanted in his chest gives him tremendous power. He uses it to save his friends when they are under attack by the Host. But the blast uses up all his energy and he dies.

DATA FILE

HOMEWORLD:
STO

SPECIAL ABILITIES:
ELECTROMAGNETIC PULSES (EMP), SQUEEZING THROUGH SMALL HOLES

DOCTORS MET:
10TH

BARBARA WRIGHT
CONSIDERATE COMPANION

Barbara is a history teacher from London and one of the Doctor's first human companions. Gentle and wise, she is determined to keep an open mind about the many alien life forms she encounters, and her knowledge of history proves invaluable whenever the TARDIS journeys into Earth's past.

DATA FILE
ORIGIN:
LONDON, ENGLAND
OCCUPATION:
HISTORY TEACHER
DOCTORS MET:
1ST

CHANGING HISTORY
When Barbara is mistaken for an Aztec goddess, she tries to use her divine status to stop the Aztec practice of human sacrifice, but is upset to find she can't change history.

Barbara teaches at Coal Hill School where the Doctor's granddaughter Susan is a pupil. Curious about the strange girl, Barbara and fellow teacher Ian Chesterton follow Susan home one night and end up being whisked off into space and time!

THE BEAST
LEGENDARY EVIL ENTITY

Before time itself existed, the Disciples of Light imprisoned a gigantic demon beneath the surface of Krop Tor. They placed the planet in perpetual orbit around a black hole, knowing that should the creature ever escape its bonds, the planet would immediately fall into the black hole, destroying the Beast in the process.

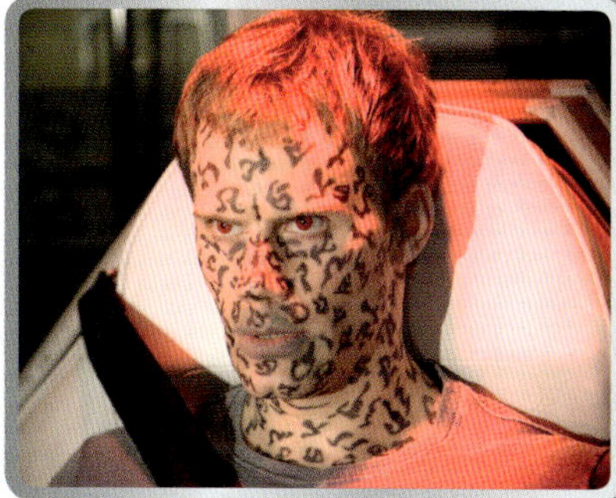

POSSESSED BY THE BEAST The Beast possesses all of the Ood on Krop Tor. And when a human expedition arrives at Sanctuary Base, it plans to escape its prison by also taking over the mind and body of crewmember Toby Zed.

FEROCIOUS APPEARANCE INSPIRED LEGENDS OF DEVILS AND EVIL ACROSS THE UNIVERSE

OVERSIZED, CURVED HORNS

DATA FILE

ORIGIN:
BEFORE TIME BEGAN

SPECIAL ABILITIES:
POSSESSION, TELEKINESIS, BREATHING FIRE

DOCTORS MET:
10TH

The Beast is defeated when Rose Tyler causes the possessed Toby Zed to be ejected into space. The black hole swallows him up, and the creature's body also perishes when Krop Tor itself is sucked into the black hole.

BEN JACKSON
COURAGEOUS COMPANION

A young cockney sailor, Ben meets the First Doctor in 1960s London and becomes caught up in WOTAN's attempt to take over the world with its lethal war machines. Practical, down-to-Earth and full of fight, Ben is not afraid of risking his own life, especially if his fellow companions are in danger.

UNINVITED GUEST
Ben's life changes forever when he and his new friend Polly follow the Doctor into the TARDIS. Ever the realist, Ben takes some convincing that he has barged aboard a space-time machine.

DATA FILE
ORIGIN:
LONDON, ENGLAND, EARTH
OCCUPATION:
ROYAL NAVY SAILOR
DOCTORS MET:
1ST, 2ND

Ben goes on some incredible adventures, fighting the likes of the Daleks, Cybermen and crab-like Macra. Eventually, the TARDIS takes him back to Earth and he is delighted to discover that he has arrived on the same day he had left!

BLACK GUARDIAN
GUARDIAN OF DARKNESS AND CHAOS

The Black Guardian is a dangerous being that thrives on evil and darkness in the universe. As powerful as the White Guardian, the Black Guardian will appear in times of great chaos. He can appear out of thin air and manipulate people so they do what he wants.

GUARDIAN AGENTS
The Black Guardian, like all Guardians, does not act directly. He has many agents who work for him, including the Shadow, a mysterious cowled figure.

BLACK BIRD HEADDRESS

ORNATE BLACK ROBES

The Black Guardian will always dress in black. However, he can change his appearance to trick people and once pretended to be the White Guardian to confuse the Doctor.

DATA FILE

HOMEWORLD:
UNKNOWN

SPECIAL ABILITIES:
SHAPE-SHIFTING, MIND CONTROL

DOCTORS MET:
4TH, 5TH

BLON FEL-FOTCH PASAMEER-DAY SLITHEEN

CALCIUM-BASED CRIMINAL

Blon is a particularly devious member of the Slitheen family. She kills MI5 officer Margaret Blaine and hides in her skin in order to infiltrate government. Her true form is an 8-foot (2.5-metre) tall green alien. Like all Slitheen, she is a wanted criminal, obsessed by money and prone to extreme flatulence.

WARMONGER

Blon tries to start World War III. When her plot fails and her entire family are blown up, she plans a nuclear meltdown in revenge.

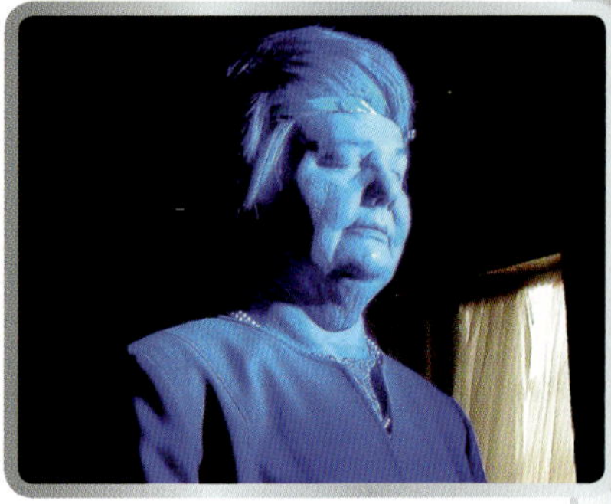

HIDDEN ZIP IN FOREHEAD

Blon was made to carry out her first kill aged thirteen. If she had refused, her father would have fed her to the Venom Grubs. She loves the thrill of hunting humans and the last thing Blon wants is to return to Raxacoricofallapatorius where she faces execution.

DATA FILE

HOMEWORLD:
RAXACORICOFALLAPATORIUS

SPECIAL ABILITIES:
HIDING AS A HUMAN, IMMENSE STRENGTH, MANIPULATION

DOCTORS MET:
9TH

HUMAN SKIN SUIT

BORUSA
CORRUPT TIME LORD

Borusa is a Time Lord, who has held various positions within the High Council on Gallifrey. At first a kind and gentle man, one of his pupils at the Prydon Academy was the Doctor, and the two Time Lords were great friends. He later regenerates into a more dangerous character.

LOVE-HATE RELATIONSHIP

Until the end, the Doctor always has great respect for Borusa – in many ways, the Doctor looks up to him. However, the Doctor is surprised to find out that his old friend would later put all his lives in danger.

EMBELLISHED HEADDRESS

DATA FILE

HOMEWORLD: GALLIFREY

SPECIAL ABILITIES: REGENERATION

DOCTORS MET: 4TH, 5TH

TIME LORD TRAP

To gain access to Rassilon's tomb, President Borusa takes various incarnations of the Doctor out of space and time and places them in the Death Zone.

As Lord President of Gallifrey, Borusa decides he wants immortality. As punishment, he is turned into living stone inside Rassilon's tomb in the Death Zone.

BRIAN WILLIAMS

RORY WILLIAMS' FATHER

Rory's dad Brian is a conservative 50-year-old with a limited world view. He hates travelling, never venturing further than the paper shop or the golf course. But all that changes when the TARDIS materialises around him and whisks him into space for an adventure with dinosaurs!

Although Brian is often critical of Rory, he is very protective of him. When pterodactyls swoop at Rory, Brian fights them off with a trowel, and he makes the Doctor promise to bring Rory and Amy back safely.

JACKET WITH MANY USEFUL POCKETS

PRACTICAL CLOTHING FOR GARDENING

TRICEY, FETCH!
Brian is staggered to find dinosaurs on a spaceship, and even more so to ride one! When the Doctor can't find a way to get the Triceratops moving, quick-thinking Brian chucks his golf balls and it runs after them.

BRIAN'S LOG
Brian's horizons are massively broadened by his space adventure. When millions of cubes appear all over Earth, Brian is full of ideas of what they might be and records his observations of them in a video log.

DATA FILE

ORIGIN:
ENGLAND, EARTH

HOBBIES:
GARDENING, DIY

DOCTORS MET:
11TH

BRIGADIER LETHBRIDGE-STEWART

FORMER COMMANDER OF UNIT

The Brigadier has been one of the Doctor's greatest allies and a close friend. The pair first meet when Lethbridge-Stewart is a Colonel and together they work to defeat the invading Great Intelligence. Some years later, the newly promoted Brigadier dedicates himself to defending Earth as head of UNIT.

NESTENE INVASION
With the Doctor as his scientific advisor, the Brigadier helps see off countless alien invasions, including an attempt by the Nestenes and the Master to conquer Earth.

DATA FILE

ORIGIN:
SCOTLAND, EARTH

OCCUPATION:
HEAD OF THE UK CONTINGENT OF UNIT

DOCTORS MET:
1ST, 2ND, 3RD, 4TH, 5TH, 7TH

UNIT
UNIT stands for Unified Intelligence Taskforce (previously United Nations Intelligence Taskforce). It is a military group set up to investigate and counter paranormal threats to Earth. A number of different incarnations of the Doctor have had close involvement with the organisation, and with Brigadier Lethbridge-Stewart.

As a military man, the Brigadier is fiercely patriotic and his first instinct is to blow up anything he sees as a threat, much to the Doctor's annoyance. Although the Doctor leaves UNIT, the pair remain friends and meet up several times.

CANTON EVERETT DELAWARE III
AGENT WITH ATTITUDE

Canton Everett Delaware III is an ex-FBI agent recruited by President Nixon to investigate some cryptic phone calls. He meets the Doctor in the Oval Office and is immediately impressed by his skills of deduction. They join forces to solve the mystery calls and fight The Silence.

MEANS BUSINESS

CLASSIC BLACK SECRET AGENT SUIT

SHOES IMPRACTICAL FOR DESERTS

FIGHTING THE SILENCE
Canton is not afraid to break the rules. He pretends to re-join the FBI to hunt down Amy, Rory and River but is actually helping them halt the Silent invasion.

DATA FILE

HOMEWORLD:
EARTH

HOBBIES:
RULE-BREAKING

DOCTORS MET:
11TH

The FBI kicked Canton out for wanting to marry a man. A rebel by nature, he takes it as a compliment when Nixon says he has a problem with authority.

LAKE SILENCIO
Canton remains loyal to the Doctor even into his old age, fulfilling one final task for him. He gives River petrol to burn the Doctor's body at Lake Silencio.

THE CAPTAIN
CYBORG PIRATE

Bad-tempered, dangerous and ruthless, the Captain is part human, part machine. He is feared on Zanak, the planet he appears to rule. Zanak can mine other worlds and drain them of their valuable mineral wealth.

STRONG, MECHANICAL ARM

PET ROBOTIC PARROT CALLED POLYPHASE AVATRON

The Captain was wounded when a spaceship he was on crashed into Zanak. One of very few survivors, he needed extensive surgery, including a replacement, cybernetic arm.

THE CAPTAIN'S NURSE
The Captain is actually controlled by the ancient Queen Xanxia. She uses the energy from ruined planets to stay alive. A projection of her appears by his side as his "nurse".

PIRATE PLANET
The Captain travels around the whole universe with his pirate planet Zanak, capturing and destroying other worlds.

DATA FILE
HOMEWORLD:
ZANAK
HOBBIES:
PIRACY, MINING, SHOUTING
DOCTORS MET:
4TH

CAPTAIN JACK HARKNESS
IMMORTAL COMPANION

Originally a Time Agent manipulating history to remove "rogue elements", Captain Jack meets the Ninth Doctor in war-torn London and joins the TARDIS crew when the Doctor saves him from his exploding spaceship. Cheeky and flirtatious, he throws himself into his adventures and helps stop a Slitheen from destroying Earth before defending Satellite Five against a Dalek invasion.

A 51st century time-travelling con man, Jack takes on the identity of an American Royal Air Force volunteer, Captain Jack Harkness, who had died in action earlier in 1941. Jack eventually ends up working for the Torchwood Institute, which protects the British Empire from extra-terrestrial threat.

1940s MILITARY COSTUME

GUN IN HOLSTER

BROWN LEATHER SHOES

DATA FILE

ORIGIN:
BOESHANE PENINSULA

OCCUPATION:
FORMER TIME AGENT AND CON MAN, TORCHWOOD AGENT

DOCTORS MET:
9TH, 10TH

LIVING FOREVER

After Jack is exterminated by the Daleks, Rose Tyler uses the power of the Time Vortex to bring him back to life, making him immortal in the process. It may be his destiny to become the Face of Boe...

IMMORTAL SKILLS

Jack's immortality makes him the perfect companion to help the Tenth Doctor when the Master conquers Earth. Jack also helps stop Davros and the Daleks from destroying the universe with their reality bomb.

CAPTAIN MIKE YATES

THE BRIGADIER'S SECOND-IN-COMMAND

Charming and easy-going, Captain Yates is the Brigadier's efficient right-hand man. Despite years of good service, his idealistic nature eventually leads to his involvement with a project that will see Earth revert to prehistoric times. Having betrayed his friends, he is allowed to take extended sick leave and resign from UNIT.

DATA FILE

ORIGIN:
ENGLAND, EARTH

OCCUPATION:
FORMER UNIT CAPTAIN

DOCTORS MET:
3RD

GIANT SPIDERS
After leaving UNIT, Yates ends up in a Buddhist meditation centre, but soon realises something is wrong when his fellow meditators make contact with the spiders of Metebelis III.

During his time at UNIT, Yates helps defend Earth against a stream of alien invaders, including the Autons, Axons and Daleks. He also goes undercover to investigate a chemical company whose pollutants have created a race of giant maggots!

CARRIONITES
SHAPE-CHANGING ALIEN WITCHES

In their true form, the Carrionites are hideous wraiths. Using a word-based science often mistaken for witchcraft, they are able to transform themselves into humanoids, and can also warp reality.

The Carrionites were once banished into the Deep Darkness. However, the grief of playwright William Shakespeare is strong enough to allow three of them to come to Earth in the late 1500s.

DATA FILE

ORIGIN:
REXEL PLANETARY CONFIGURATION

SPECIAL ABILITIES:
SHAPE-CHANGING, MANIPULATING MATTER USING WORDS

DOCTORS MET:
10TH

ESCAPE ATTEMPT

During the performance of one of Shakespeare's plays, three Carrionites use their "magic" to help the rest of their kind descend to Earth. They want to destroy the entire human race.

WILLIAM SHAKESPEARE

Just as it is Shakespeare who brings the Carrionites to Earth, it is his combination of words that sends them back into the Darkness. The three on Earth become trapped in their own crystal ball, which the Doctor decides to keep aboard the TARDIS for safekeeping.

CELESTIAL TOYMAKER
DANGEROUS GAME PLAYER

A mysterious figure, the Celestial Toymaker has lived forever in a strange world outside of the known universe. The Toymaker sets people challenges through a series of childish and potentially fatal games. If a player loses, they become trapped in the Toymaker's world for the rest of time.

DRIVEN TO INSANITY BY PROLONGED ISOLATION

CHINESE MANDARIN STYLE CLOTHES

DATA FILE

HOMEWORLD:
OUTSIDE SPACE AND TIME

SPECIAL ABILITIES:
IMMORTALITY, ANIMATING TOYS, TURNING PEOPLE INVISIBLE

DOCTORS MET:
1st

The Celestial Toymaker cheats, lies and does not like to lose. He makes it difficult for players to leave his world – and losers become his toys.

HELPING HAND
Two dolls, Clara and Joey, are brought to life by the Toymaker to help him with his traps. They play games with the Doctor and his companions.

SINISTER GAMES
The Doctor's companions Dodo and Steven find themselves playing for their lives – including a game of deadly musical chairs and electrified hopscotch.

CLARA
THAT IMPOSSIBLE GIRL

Clara is an enigma. She appears as both a posh Victorian governess and a Cockney barmaid. In the far future, an identical girl called Oswin Oswald crashes *The Alaska* ship on an Asylum planet and becomes a Dalek. They look the same and say the same phrase to the Doctor hundreds of years apart.

TERRIBLE TRUTH
Oswin Oswald is the sole member of the *Alaska* crew not converted into a Dalek puppet. She is so intelligent that the Daleks perform a full conversion on her. Unable to face the horror of what she has become, she lives in a dream world. But when the Doctor confronts her with the truth, her Dalek nature takes over.

Clara is smart, sassy and determined. She tracks down the Doctor and refuses to leave until he explains who he is.

VICTORIAN ERA BARMAID OUTFIT

IMPOSSIBLE CLARA
The Doctor finds Clara maddening and intriguing in equal measure. She helps him fight alien snowmen and would have become his companion if she hadn't been killed by the Ice Governess.

DATA FILE

ORIGIN:
EARTH

SPECIAL ABILITIES:
SMART, HEADSTRONG, MAKER OF SOUFFLÉS

DOCTORS MET:
11TH

CRAIG OWENS
THE DOCTOR'S LANDLORD

Craig Owens is a call centre worker, married to Sophie and father to baby Alfie (aka Stormageddon). He becomes friends with the Eleventh Doctor when the Time Lord moves in as his lodger. Together they fight an alien spaceship disguised as the top half of Craig's house, and stop a Cyber invasion.

Dubbed "Mr Sofa Man" by the Doctor, Craig hates travelling. But, of all his friends, it's Craig that the Doctor visits before he is due to die at Lake Silencio. The two are very close and both like to use the phrase "geronimo".

COSY CARDIGAN

COMFORTABLE TROUSERS FOR WATCHING TV

AVATAR ATTACK!
Initially too shy to tell Sophie he has a crush on her, Craig declares his love for her while fighting the spaceship's avatar. Their kiss causes the ship to implode!

CYBER CONVERSION
Craig is a loyal friend to the Doctor. He even attempts to rescue him from the Cybermen and is almost converted into a Cyber Controller in the process.

DATA FILE

ORIGIN:
ENGLAND, EARTH

SPECIAL ABILITIES:
FIGHTING CYBERMATS, EXPLODING CYBERMEN

DOCTORS MET:
11TH

CYBERMEN

STEEL SOLDIERS

Cybermen are one of the Doctor's most enduring enemies. They are near indestructible cybernetic beings with living brains jammed into metal bodies. Inside their super-strong casings, an emotional inhibitor suppresses all human feelings. They have one goal – to upgrade all other beings into Cyberkind.

DATA FILE

HOMEWORLD:
MONDAS,
PARALLEL EARTH

SPECIAL ABILITIES:
LONG-LIFE, EXTREME STRENGTH, HANDS THAT CAN ELECTROCUTE

DOCTORS MET:
1st, 2nd, 3rd, 4th, 5th, 6th, 7th, 10th, 11th

ENORMOUS STRENGTH AND POWER

METAL EXOSKELETON

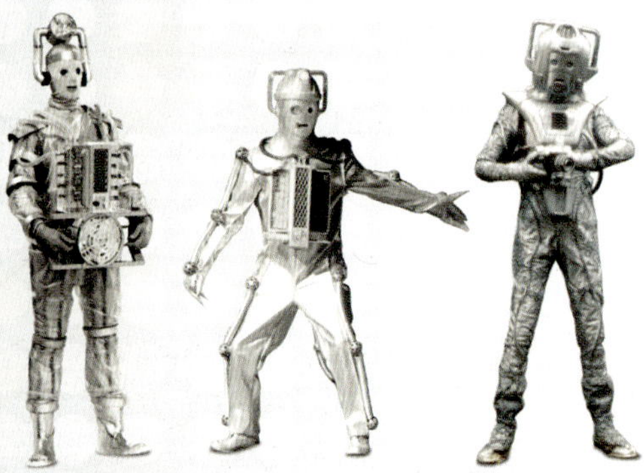

The first Cybermen came from the planet Mondas and had cloth faces and human hands. Their shape has evolved repeatedly.

PARALLEL-EARTH CYBERMEN

A new army of deadly Cybermen is created on a parallel Earth by Cybus Industries' owner, John Lumic. They believe they are Human Point Two and everyone must become like them.

CYBERKING

CYBERSHADE

In 1851, Cybermen built the CyberKing – a massive, dreadnought-class battleship – and also experimented on animals to create Cybershades.

Cybermen relentlessly seek to upgrade themselves and mankind, and are merciless to those who refuse. Chanting "Delete!", they electrocute victims with their hands or blast them with lasers.

DALEKS

THE DOCTOR'S DEADLIEST ENEMY

Daleks are the stuff of nightmares. Inside their almost indestructible dalekanium shells lies a foul one-eyed Kaled mutant. Genetically engineered by Davros to be empty of all emotions but hate, they seek to destroy all other "less superior" life forms, and electrocute their victims with the terrifying cry of "EXTERMINATE"!

The animosity between the Daleks and the Doctor predates the Time War that apparently destroyed all Time Lords and Daleks. The Daleks both hate and fear the Doctor, calling him "the Oncoming Storm" and "the Predator".

DATA FILE

HOMEWORLD:
SKARO

SPECIAL ABILITIES:
EXTERMINATING, EXTRACTING DATA FROM HUMAN MINDS

DOCTORS MET:
ALL

The Daleks have assumed many guises over the years. The Doctor has fought many types, including:

ORIGINAL DALEK

IRONSIDE

DALEK SEC

THE SUPREME

DALEK PARLIAMENT

When the Daleks summon the Doctor before the Dalek Parliament, they hope to use him then destroy him. But Oswin Oswald erases their databases, leaving the Doctor's archenemies with no memories of him!

DAVROS
CREATOR OF THE DALEKS

A crippled and deranged scientist, Davros is obsessed with the survival of his race, the Kaleds, following centuries of chemical and nuclear warfare. He creates the Daleks and programmes them with the instinct to destroy all other life forms in the universe.

DALEK DESTRUCTION
When the Tenth Doctor destroys all the Daleks, Davros is left burning. The Doctor offers to save him, but bitter Davros declines, believing the Doctor to be "The Destroyer of Worlds".

REALITY BOMB
Davros comes up with crazy schemes, such as his construction of a massive reality bomb. He plans to use the bomb to destroy all matter in the universe, leaving nothing but the Daleks and himself.

Davros has an uneasy relationship with his own pitiless creations. The Daleks once tried to kill him, believing in their own superiority. But when their own survival is threatened they often return to him for help.

DATA FILE

HOMEWORLD:
SKARO

SPECIAL ABILITIES:
CAN FIRE ENERGY BOLTS FROM HIS FINGERTIPS

DOCTORS MET:
4TH, 5TH, 6TH, 7TH, 10TH

THE FIRST DOCTOR
TARDIS THIEF

The Doctor is a Time Lord, an extra-terrestrial leader from the planet Gallifrey, who travels through space and time. He is part-warrior, part-conflict resolver. The First Doctor is a tetchy, eccentric old man who steals a TARDIS (time machine) and travels through the universe. Occasionally stubborn, aloof and absent-minded, he mellows as he gets used to travelling with a succession of long-suffering human companions.

The Doctor regenerates, or transforms, when his body becomes old or mortally wounded. This changes him physically and alters his personality. After an epic battle, the First Doctor announces that his old body has at last worn out. His features change into those of a much younger man!

AZTEC LOVE

Cameca is an Aztec lady to whom the Doctor unknowingly proposes in the 15th century. She is the Doctor's first known love interest.

DEFEATING THE DALEKS

The Doctor first meets the Daleks when he accidentally lands the TARDIS on Skaro, where the ruthless Daleks are planning to wipe out their enemies, the Thals.

MONOCLE

DATA FILE

SPECIAL ABILITIES:
POWER OF HYPNOSIS (WITH THE HELP OF HIS SIGNET RING)

REASON FOR REGENERATING:
EXHAUSTION AND OLD AGE

THE SECOND DOCTOR
CUNNING CLOWN

Compared with the stern figure of the First Doctor, the Second Doctor is more like a dotty uncle. He bumbles around and often panics in dangerous situations. His nature often fools his enemies into underestimating him – he has the same razor-sharp intelligence as ever before.

DOCTOR ON TRIAL
The Time Lords finally catch up with the Second Doctor and put him on trial for interfering in galactic affairs. As punishment, he is forced to regenerate and live as an exile on planet Earth.

RECORDER

TARTAN TROUSERS

DATA FILE

INTERESTS:
PLAYING THE RECORDER

REASONS FOR REGENERATION:
FORCED TO CHANGE HIS APPEARANCE BY THE TIME LORDS

CYBER RISING
It is in this incarnation that the Doctor first encounters the Cyber Controller and Cybermats, deep within the Cyber-Tombs on the planet Telos. With the help of Jamie and Victoria, the Doctor fights off what are believed to be the very last of the Cybermen.

The Second Doctor believes it is his duty to fight the many evils in the universe. In his time he battles both Cybermen and Daleks, the robotic Yeti and the reptilian Ice Warriors – he even encounters a scary seaweed creature.

THE THIRD DOCTOR
EARTH EXILE

Charming and flamboyant, this version of the Doctor is a dashing action hero with a fondness for fast vehicles and cool gadgets. During his exile, he reluctantly joins UNIT as its scientific advisor, but he soon tires of defending Earth against alien invaders and longs to roam the universe once more.

DOCTOR TIMES THREE
When the Time Lords come under attack, they bring the first three Doctors together to help save them. As a reward, the Third Doctor's exile is finally lifted.

DATA FILE
INTERESTS: VENUSIAN AIKIDO
REASONS FOR REGENERATION: RADIATION SICKNESS

Alongside Brigadier Lethbridge-Stewart and companions Liz Shaw, Jo Grant and Sarah Jane Smith, the Third Doctor fights various menaces from Autons to Axons and dinosaurs to Daleks. He also battles the Master who is as determined as ever to destroy humanity.

SPIDER DOOM
The Third Doctor's life ends when he and Sarah Jane run into giant spiders on Metebelis III. In the course of confronting the eight limbed Great One, the Doctor consumes a lethal amount of radiation, triggering his regeneration.

THE FOURTH DOCTOR
EAGER EXPLORER

At times madly eccentric, at others mysterious and moody, the Fourth Doctor is the most unpredictable. He has a wild spirit of adventure, an offbeat sense of humour and loves filling his pockets with random objects.

DOCTOR ASSASSIN
Freed from his exile on Earth, the Fourth Doctor is able to travel the universe once more. He is even summoned back to Gallifrey, where he apparently steals some ceremonial Time Lord robes and murders the Time Lord President – before it is revealed to have all been another of the Master's plots.

A DOCTOR'S DILEMMA
This Doctor has the chance to destroy the Daleks at the point of their creation. He struggles with the decision, questioning if he has the right to commit genocide.

Some of the Fourth Doctor's closest companions are Sarah Jane Smith, the savage Leela and Time Lady Romana. He saves Gallifrey from the invading Sontarans and also goes on an epic mission to assemble the Key to Time, restoring harmony to the universe.

DATA FILE
INTERESTS:
YO-YO TRICKS

REASON FOR REGENERATION:
FALLS FROM THE TOP OF AN ENORMOUS RADIO TELESCOPE

THE FIFTH DOCTOR

PEACE-SEEKING PACIFIST

With his love of cricket, the younger-looking Fifth Doctor possesses a manic, nervous energy, which often leads him to rush about and talk too fast, while his vulnerable nature means he occasionally doubts himself. But when faced with a dangerous enemy, he is every bit as determined and heroic as his previous selves.

DATA FILE

INTERESTS:
PLAYING CRICKET

REASON FOR REGENERATION:
SPECTROX TOXAEMIA

The Fifth Doctor becomes close to his companions, including the gentle Nyssa, stroppy flight attendant Tegan and Turlough – a Black Guardian agent who is secretly out to kill him. He is deeply upset by the tragic loss of young Adric, who dies while trying to save Earth.

NOBLE SACRIFICE
The Doctor and his companion Peri Brown contract an illness called spectrox toxaemia on Androzani Minor. The Doctor gives up his share of the cure to save her life, but as a result he regenerates for the fifth time.

FIVE DOCTORS
As part of a cruel game organised by the Time Lord Rassilon, all five incarnations of the Doctor meet in order to save their past, present and future lives. The Fifth Doctor is offered the position of President of Gallifrey for the role he plays, but prefers to return to a life of travelling.

THE SIXTH DOCTOR
COLOURFUL CHARACTER

Stubborn, self-centred, with a loud manner and even louder dress sense, the Sixth Doctor is difficult to like at first. Happily, though, his dedication to fighting evil remains as strong as ever, and the more extreme aspects of his personality mellow as time goes by, revealing a surprisingly caring Doctor beneath the bluster.

DATA FILE

INTERESTS:
ENJOYS RECITING POETRY

REASONS FOR REGENERATION:
THE RANI'S LASER ATTACK ON THE TARDIS

The Sixth Doctor travels with botany student Peri and computer expert Mel. As well as Daleks and Cybermen, he fights the slug-like Gastropods and the money-loving Mentors, until he meets his end at the hands of the Rani.

ON TRIAL AGAIN

The Doctor has faced being prosecuted on more than one occassion and in several incarnations. The Sixth Doctor faces a dark version of himself in the shape of the villainous Valeyard.

DOCTOR TIMES TWO

The Sixth Doctor has to rescue the Second Doctor, who has been kidnapped by the Sontarans and Androgums. They want to operate on him to discover the secret of time travel!

THE SEVENTH DOCTOR
DARKER DOCTOR

As eccentric as any of his predecessors, the Seventh Doctor is a wiry, off-the-wall character at first, given to acting the clown and spouting mangled proverbs. Over time, though, he reveals a darker side to his nature, coming across as a master chess-player, who is forever one step ahead of his enemies.

QUESTION MARK-SHAPED UMBRELLA USED TO DISARM FOES

PATTERNED CLOTHES DISGUISE DARKER NATURE

BROWN AND WHITE BROGUES WORN BENEATH TWEED TROUSERS

DATA FILE

INTERESTS:
PLAYING THE SPOONS, MAGIC TRICKS, CHESS

REASONS FOR REGENERATION:
BULLET WOUNDS AND SUBSEQUENT HEART SURGERY

The Seventh Doctor's closest friend is a rebellious teenager called Ace. He enjoys educating her as they travel the universe fighting menaces such as Cybermen, Cheetah people, Husks and Haemovores. However, he is not opposed to manipulating her to get his own way.

DALEK DESTROYER

After allowing Davros to steal a deadly device called the Hand of Omega, the Seventh Doctor tricks him into activating it. The pre-programmed Hand then destroys Skaro, the Daleks' homeworld!

UNITED

The Seventh Doctor is pleased to be reunited with an old friend when the Brigadier comes out of retirement to help UNIT deal with an alien invasion.

THE EIGHTH DOCTOR
PARADOXICAL PSYCHIC

A more human version of the Doctor, this eighth incarnation has a childlike playfulness coupled with an infectious zest for life and adventure. Warm, witty and charming, he also has the uncanny knack of being able to predict events in people's personal futures – a talent none of his other selves has possessed.

BATTLING THE MASTER
The Eighth Doctor has to fight for his life when the Master attempts to steal his remaining regenerations. In the end, his deadly enemy is absorbed into the TARDIS's power source.

Following his regeneration, the Eighth Doctor steals a fancy dress costume to wear, which is similar to the clothes worn by 19th century gunfighter Wild Bill Hickok.

19TH CENTURY-LOOKING VELVET JACKET

EMBROIDERED WAISTCOAT

SAVING GRACE
This Doctor is assisted by Grace Holloway, a heart surgeon who had tried to operate on the Seventh Doctor.

DATA FILE
SPECIAL ABILITIES: PREDICTING THE FUTURE
REASON FOR REGENERATING: UNKNOWN

THE NINTH DOCTOR
WAR-WEARY WANDERER

The Ninth Doctor is left emotionally scarred in the aftermath of the Time War, a catastrophic event in which the Time Lords are destroyed. As the last of his kind, this Doctor needs a human companion more than ever before, and is relieved to meet Rose Tyler, a feisty shop-girl from London.

SONIC SCREWDRIVER

WELL-WORN LEATHER JACKET

DATA FILE

SPECIAL ABILITIES:
INCREDIBLE TIMING – HE ONCE MANAGED TO STEP THROUGH THE BLADES OF A MASSIVE SPINNING FAN

REASON FOR REGENERATING:
CELLULAR DEGENERATION AFTER ABSORBING THE TIME VORTEX

This Doctor deals ruthlessly with his enemies if they choose not to heed his warnings. He refuses to save the villainous Cassandra, launches a missile attack against the Slitheen and even orders the last Dalek in the universe to destroy itself.

ACQUIRING ASSISTANCE
The Doctor acquires a new companion when he travels back to World War II. Captain Jack Harkness is a con man from the 51st century dressed as an air force pilot.

SAVING ROSE
When Rose absorbs the whole of the Time Vortex, the Ninth Doctor bravely draws it into his own body to save her life, knowing full well it would trigger a regeneration.

THE TENTH DOCTOR
LAID-BACK LONER

This version of the Doctor is empathetic, confident and quirky, with a real zest for adventure. More talkative and laid-back than his predecessor, he revels in his voyages through space and time. Towards the end of his life, though, he grows sad at the loss of so many friends, and decides to travel alone once more.

OLD TIMER
As a warning to Martha and humanity, the Master uses his laser screwdriver to age the Doctor's body to his real age of over 900!

SONIC SCREWDRIVER USED FOR PICKING LOCKS, REMOTELY CONTROLLING OTHER DEVICES AND TRACKING ALIENS

BROWN PINSTRIPE SUIT

SCRUFFY PLIMSOLES

With his loyal companions, the Tenth Doctor battles an array of adversaries, from Cat Nuns and Carrionites to the Sycorax and Sontarans. He even manages to stop the Time Lord Rassilon's attempt to bring about the end of time itself after he was previously assumed killed in the Time War.

FAREWELL ROSE
One of the Tenth Doctor's toughest moments is saying goodbye to Rose at Bad Wolf Bay. She becomes trapped in a parallel universe and he believes he has lost her forever.

DATA FILE

SPECIAL ABILITIES:
CAN ANALYSE SUBSTANCES BY TASTING THEM

REASON FOR REGENERATING:
RADIATION POISONING

THE ELEVENTH DOCTOR
BABY-FACED BRAINIAC

The most youthful-looking Doctor of all, the Eleventh Doctor has one of the most alien and eccentric personas yet. Like an excitable kid at times, he doesn't always appear to take dangerous situations seriously, but when confronting his enemies, he is capable of showing a colder, and even ruthless, side to his nature.

BIG BANG TWO

When the universe all but collapses, the Eleventh Doctor achieves the impossible – he flies the Pandorica prison box at his exploding TARDIS, miraculously managing to reboot the entire universe!

DATA FILE

INTERESTS: PLAYING FOOTBALL

REASON FOR REGENERATING: HAS NOT YET REGENERATED

DOCTOR SOLO

Following the loss of Amy and Rory, the Eleventh Doctor continues adventuring with new companion Clara, knowing how dangerous it is for him to travel alone.

This incarnation of the Doctor faces greater challenges than ever before. His biggest enemy is The Silence, a religious order that is desperate to prevent the revelation of the Doctor's real name – something known by very few people, one of whom is River Song.

DOCTOR SIMEON

SERVANT OF THE GREAT INTELLIGENCE

As a child, Walter Simeon's only friend is the snowman he makes in his garden. Walter pours his darkest dreams into it and they become telepathically linked. As an adult, Doctor Simeon sets up the GI Institute and becomes the devoted servant of a disembodied alien called the Great Intelligence.

TOP HAT

MERCILESS AND EMOTIONLESS

DEVOTED TO HIS MASTER

FUR-LINED COAT FOR STAYING WARM IN SNOWY CLIMES

Ruthless to his core, Doctor Simeon thinks nothing of feeding his workers to the savage Snowmen. He gathers alien ice samples from all over London to help his master learn about Earth.

CARNIVOROUS SNOWMEN
The Great Intelligence is an extremely powerful alien who longs to take human form. Using carnivorous alien snow, it plans to create a world full of living ice people.

ICE COLD
When his mind is erased by a Memory Worm, Doctor Simeon becomes possessed by the Great Intelligence and transforms into an ice-faced zombie who tries to freeze the Doctor.

DATA FILE

ORIGIN:
EARTH

SPECIAL ABILITIES:
PSYCHIC LINK WITH THE GREAT INTELLIGENCE

DOCTORS MET:
11TH

DONNA NOBLE
TEMPERAMENTAL COMPANION

Funny, feisty and fiery-tempered, Donna is one of the Doctor's more outspoken companions. She adores travelling in the TARDIS – even though she once believed she'd never be able to cope with the Doctor's dangerous lifestyle – and her incredible adventures open up her mind to the wonders of the universe.

DATA FILE

ORIGIN:
LONDON, EARTH

OCCUPATION:
OFFICE TEMP

DOCTORS MET:
10TH

During a battle with the Daleks, Donna is transformed by the Doctor's regeneration energy, which gives her the consciousness of a Time Lord. She uses her new-found great intelligence to save the universe from Davros's reality bomb!

SPACE BRIDE

Donna first meets the Doctor when she is accidentally transported into his TARDIS on her wedding day. She initially declines his invitation to join him on his travels, but soon realises that her ordinary, everyday life is dull in comparison.

DOCTOR DONNA

Tragically, the Time Lord part of Donna's brain is too much for her and the Doctor is forced to erase her mind in order to save her life. He takes her back to Earth, where she eventually meets and marries her husband, Shaun Temple.

DORIUM MALDOVAR
BLUE-SKINNED BAR OWNER

A big blue alien of dubious morals, Dorium owns a space bar called the Maldovarium in the 51st century. He dabbles in the black market and sells the Headless Monks security software with which to kidnap Amy Pond. Dorium is always in the know.

The Doctor summons Dorium to repay a debt by helping him rescue Amy from Demon's Run. But he is killed by Headless Monks and his head is placed in the Labyrinth of Skulls.

SILENCE WILL FALL
Although bodiless, Dorium's head remains well-informed. He provides the Doctor with data on The Silence and reveals to him the question that must never be answered on the fields of Trenzalore.

DATA FILE
HOMEWORLD: UNKNOWN
SPECIAL FEATURES: WI-FI FITTED TO MEDIA CHIP IN HEAD
DOCTORS MET: 11th

DOROTHEA CHAPLET
CHEERFUL COMPANION

Dorothea Chaplet (nicknamed "Dodo" at school) becomes the First Doctor's companion by chance after stumbling into the TARDIS, thinking it is a real police box. Fun-loving and carefree, she has few qualms about joining the Doctor, who took something of a shine to her, thanks to her striking resemblance to his granddaughter Susan Foreman.

BEARS RESEMBLANCE TO SUSAN FOREMAN

SMART WOOL COAT

AMAZING ADVENTURES
Dodo's time with the Doctor is short, but during her travels she visits a giant space ark, fights against the evil Toymaker, and even sees her dream come true when she meets legendary lawman Wyatt Earp in the Wild West!

In one of Dodo's more frightening exploits, her mind was taken over by the mad supercomputer WOTAN. The Doctor successfully breaks its hypnotic control, but after recovering from the ordeal, Dodo decides to stay on Earth.

DATA FILE

ORIGIN:
ENGLAND, EARTH

INTERESTS:
THE WILD WEST

DOCTORS MET:
1ST

DRACONIANS
HUMANOID REPTILES

The Draconians are an intelligent, civilised and honourable race of reptilian humanoid creatures. In the 26th century, as the Earth and Draconian Empires expanded, a misunderstanding led to a war between the two races. Separate borders were agreed – creating a frontier in space.

The Draconians are ruled by an Emperor. They wear long, green robes. In the 26th century, people cruelly nicknamed them "dragons".

MASTER PLANS
In 2540, the Master and the Daleks attempt to cause another war between the two empires. They fail thanks to help from the Doctor.

THE DOCTOR AND THE DRACONIAN
There is an old Draconian legend about a man who helped the 15th Emperor at a time of great trouble during a space plague. This man was the Doctor.

DATA FILE

HOMEWORLD:
DRACONIA

PERSONALITY TRAITS:
HONESTY, HONOUR

DOCTORS MET:
3RD

THE DREAM LORD

THE DOCTOR'S DARK ALTER-EGO

The Dream Lord is created when specks of psychic pollen from Karass Don Slava become trapped in the TARDIS's time rotor. A mind parasite, the pollen feeds on the dark areas of people's psyche and it uses the Doctor's mind to create a villainous version of the Time Lord.

DANGEROUS AND MISCHIEVOUS MIND

CLOTHES REFLECT THE ELEVENTH DOCTOR'S STYLE

INVADING THE TARDIS
Appearing in the TARDIS, the Dream Lord asks the Doctor, Amy and Rory to choose which of two worlds is real, and which is only a dream. The wrong choice will kill them!

DIFFICULT CHOICES
The Dream Lord's two worlds are equally unattractive: freezing to death in a TARDIS slowly spinning into a cold star, or being obliterated by the alien Eknodines. When Rory is killed, it is at first unclear whether he will also be dead in the real world.

Taunted by the Dream Lord, the Doctor eventually realises that neither world is real and wakes up safely back in the TARDIS. The Dream Lord is defeated, but the Doctor catches one last glimpse of him, reflected in the TARDIS console...

DATA FILE

ORIGIN:
THE DOCTOR'S MIND

SPECIAL ABILITIES:
CONTROLLING PEOPLE'S DREAMS

DOCTORS MET:
11TH

EKNODINES

POSSESSED PENSIONERS

A proud and ancient race of creatures who were driven from their planet by upstart neighbours, the Eknodines flee to Earth and take possession of the elderly residents of Rory Williams' hometown Leadworth. A single green eyeball hides in the mouths of their human hosts.

LIVES INSIDE PENSIONER FROM UPPER LEADWORTH'S OLD PEOPLE'S HOME

HUMAN HOST MRS HAMIL'S BODY AND CLOTHING

FRAIL APPEARANCE HIDES GREAT STRENGTH

DATA FILE

HOMEWORLD:
UNKNOWN

SPECIAL ABILITIES:
DISGUISE, STRENGTH, DEADLY VENOM

DOCTORS MET:
11TH

JUST A DREAM

The Doctor, Amy and Rory encounter the Eknodines in a dream world conjured up by the mischievous Dream Lord. Whether they exist in reality somewhere in the universe is unknown.

VENGEANCE

Bitter at their own destruction, the Eknodines plan to do the same to other races, starting with mankind. Their eyeballs squirt out venom that can reduce a human to dust in seconds.

The Eknodines have been living in the bodies of pensioners for many years, unnaturally prolonging their lifespan. They look old and frail but are actually very strong, effortlessly picking up humans and throwing them aside.

THE FACE OF BOE
THE LAST OF BOE-KIND

A huge head in a glass tank, the Face of Boe is a mysterious being who is believed to be billions of years old. It is said that he has watched the universe grow old and that one day, just before his death, he will reveal a great secret to a lonely wanderer.

DATA FILE
ORIGIN:
THE SILVER DEVASTATION

SPECIAL ABILITIES:
TELEPATHY, SELF TELEPORTATION

DOCTORS MET:
9TH, 10TH

MESSAGE FOR THE DOCTOR
Sacrificing himself to save the people of New Earth, the Face of Boe's dying words are "you are not alone" – a warning that the Doctor's archenemy, the Master, is still alive.

The Face of Boe can teleport himself through the power of his will. He mostly grunts but is also able to communicate telepathically, and in his dying days, sings ancient songs in the mind of his devoted cat nurse, Novice Hame.

THE FAMILY OF BLOOD

GREEN, GASEOUS ALIENS

The Family of Blood are gaseous beings with short life spans. They go after the Doctor, realising his Time Lord essence will enable them to live for much longer. Following him to England in 1913, they take over the bodies of four local people and use their own keen sense of smell to hunt him down.

After hiding away in human form, the Doctor eventually confronts the Family and their soldiers, the Scarecrows, and pretends to surrender. In reality, he has tricked them into letting him rig their ship to blow itself up!

ETERNAL PUNISHMENT

The Doctor devises prisons for each member of the Family. He binds Father of Mine in unbreakable chains, freezes Son of Mine in time, throws Mother of Mine into a collapsing galaxy and traps Sister of Mine in every existing mirror!

DATA FILE

ORIGIN:
UNKNOWN

SPECIAL ABILITIES:
ACUTE SENSE OF SMELL, TAKING OVER OTHER LIFE FORMS

DOCTORS MET:
10TH

FENRIC
ANCIENT EVIL

Fenric is the name given to a powerful force as old as the universe. In the third century AD, the Doctor manages to trap Fenric inside a flask after winning a game of chess. Despite being imprisoned, Fenric is still able to use his Haemovores and manipulated humans to help with his eventual escape thousands of years later.

STOLEN BODY OF MATHEMATICIAN DR JUDSON

WORLD WAR II ERA WHEELCHAIR

CAPTAIN SORIN
The Russian soldier Captain Sorin is on a mission to steal a code-breaking machine during World War II when he becomes Fenric's latest victim. But Fenric's possession ends when the Haemovores turn on him and destroy him.

DATA FILE

ORIGIN:
THE DAWN OF TIME

SPECIAL ABILITIES:
POSSESSING PEOPLE'S BODIES

DOCTORS MET:
7TH

In Norse mythology, "Fenrir" is a wolflike figure that will destroy the world. This ancient curse is passed down through generations, as the flask carrying his being is buried in an English village by the Vikings. Fenric continues to use people as his pawns until he escapes, at which point he kills and possesses the first person he finds – the wheelchair-bound Dr Judson.

THE FLOOD
WATERY MARS MONSTERS

A highly contagious viral lifeform found in the water on Mars, the Flood was possibly once frozen under the planet's surface by the Ice Warriors. When an exploratory mission to colonise the red planet uses the water from a contaminated ice field, the Flood possess the crew.

The Flood virus is highly contagious. If just one drop of infected water touches your skin you will become one of them. Human beings are about 60 per cent water, making them the perfect host.

CONTAMINATED CARROT

The crew of Bowie Base One catch the Flood virus when their Bio-Dome becomes contaminated by Flood-infected water. One bite of a carrot turns crewmember Andy into a Flood monster and he starts converting the rest of the humans.

A NEAR ESCAPE

Six members of Bowie Base One become Flood. The Doctor and Captain Adelaide Brooke are among the few to escape infection. They know that the only way to stop the Flood reaching Earth is to blow up the base.

DATA FILE

HOMEWORLD:
MARS

SPECIAL ABILITIES:
WATER-SPRAYING, CONVERTING OTHERS, HIVE MIND

DOCTORS MET:
10TH

FUTUREKIND

SAVAGE CANNIBALS

Near the end of the universe, in the year one hundred trillion, a wild, snarling race called the Futurekind appear on the planet Malcassairo. The Futurekind resemble humans, but have developed fangs to help them slice through human flesh – their favourite food – and mark their faces with tribal patterns and metal piercings.

BRAVE CHANTHO

In an attempt to kill the Doctor, the Master lowers the defences of the Silo to let the Futurekind in. His assistant Chantho, the last of the Malmooth, tries to stop him, but the Master kills her and the Futurekind stream inside.

"HUUUUMAN!"

On their arrival on Malcassairo, the Doctor, Martha and Jack encounter the Futurekind chasing a terrified human called Padra. The only way to escape them is by running to the safety of Silo 16 – the desginated safe zone for non-Futurekind on Malcassairo.

FILTHY HAIR

FACES PAINTED WITH WOAD

The Futurekind are a primitive race who communicate using a basic hissing language. They are led by a Chieftain and hunt as a pack, yelling bloodthirsty war cries as they chase their prey.

DATA FILE

HOMEWORLD:
MALCASSAIRO

SPECIAL ABILITIES:
HUNTING, RUNNING, EATING RAW FLESH

DOCTORS MET:
10TH

GANGERS

LIVING FLESH MONSTERS

In the 22nd century, cloned body doubles are used to perform tasks that are too dangerous for humans. These Gangers look exactly like their human controllers, but are made from programmable matter called Flesh. Humans think Gangers don't feel pain, but they can, and they are determined to live a normal existence.

WAXY, BLOODSHOT FACE

MORPETH JETSAN UNIFORM

UNSTABLE FORM OF JENNIFER LUCAS' GANGER

DATA FILE

ORIGIN:
EARTH

SPECIAL ABILITIES:
COPYING HUMANS, MUTATION, STRETCHY BODIES

DOCTORS MET:
11TH

Gangers are consumed by rage and a desire to punish mankind for their ill-treatment at their hands. This is especially true for Jennifer Lucas' Ganger, which mutates into a massive human-gobbling monster!

DOCTOR GANGER

A Ganger of the Doctor is created during a solar storm. Amy is disturbed by it, believing it to be inferior, not realising the two Doctors have actually swapped places.

TRICKED TWICE

Gangers make such convincing copies that even the Doctor is fooled when Amy is swapped for one. The mysterious Madame Kovarian plays the same trick on the real Amy, kidnapping and replacing her baby with a Ganger.

GELTH

BODYSNATCHING GAS CREATURES

Having lost their bodies in the Time War, some of the gaseous Gelth use the Cardiff space-time rift to come to 19th-century Earth. They want a physical form once more, and convince the Doctor to allow them to come through in force so they can possess the bodies of dead people.

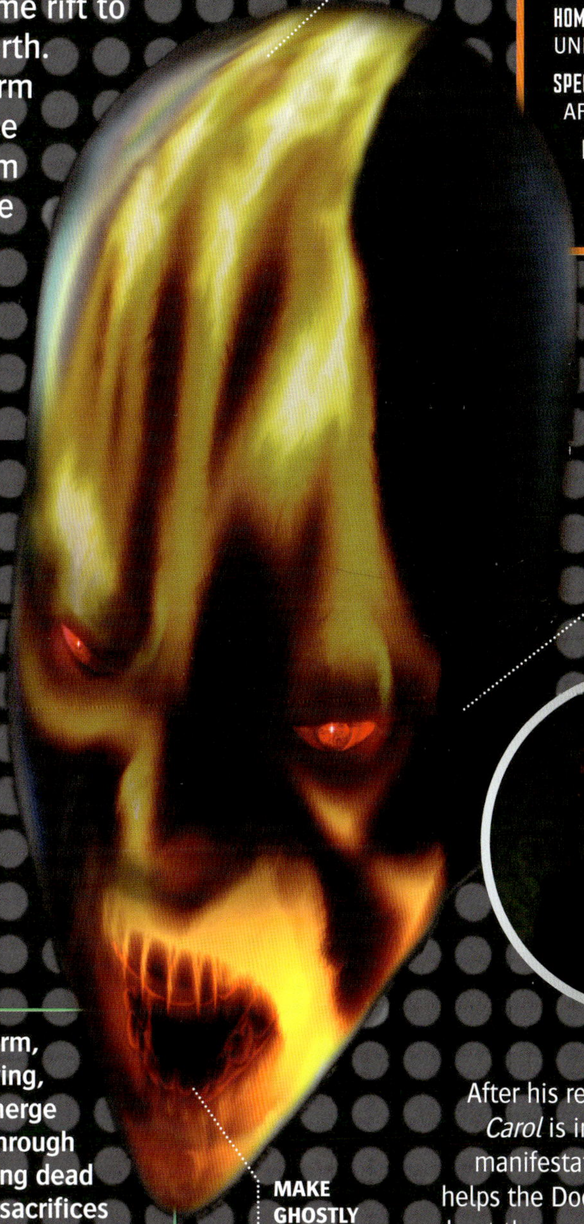

DATA FILE

HOMEWORLD: UNKNOWN

SPECIAL ABILITIES: AFFINITY WITH GAS

DOCTORS MET: 9TH

GELTH INVASION
Using psychic maid Gwyneth as a gateway, billions of Gelth begin to descend to Earth. They reveal they are planning to kill the human race and take over their corpses!

In their disembodied form, the Gelth are glowing, wraithlike beings. They emerge from gas pipes and swirl through the air before entering dead people's bodies. Gwyneth sacrifices herself by causing an enormous explosion that destroys the Gelth.

CHARLES DICKENS
After his reading of *A Christmas Carol* is interrupted by a Gelth manifestation, Charles Dickens helps the Doctor to discover more about the creatures. He even takes part in a séance, during which the Gelth reveal their plight.

GIANT MAGGOTS
LARGE INFECTED GRUBS

Huge giant maggots are the result of pollution from Global Chemicals' factory in Wales. Feeding on the slimy green chemical waste causes ordinary maggots to dramatically increase in size and become deadly. Their bite and touch infects humans, causing the victim to glow bright green and eventually die.

Found in a coal mine in Wales, the maggots are virtually indestructible. Bullets and fire do not have any effect on them. However, they are susceptible to a type of edible fungus discovered by Professor Clifford Jones.

MAGGOT MISSION
The Doctor pulls in the help of UNIT and the RAF to destroy the maggots. Like a normal maggot, the larvae creatures will turn into flies – giant flies. Only one transforms and is downed by the Doctor's cape.

DATA FILE
ORIGIN:
EARTH

SPECIAL ABILITIES:
INFECTING OTHERS, METAMORPHOSIS

DOCTORS MET:
3RD

GODS OF RAGNAROK
ENTERTAINMENT SEEKERS

Easily bored and hard to please, the Gods of Ragnarok crave one thing – entertainment. If they are not happy with what they see, they become angry and kill. They take over the Psychic Circus, also called "The Greatest Show in the Galaxy", and make people perform for their lives. Creepy clowns and robots help organise talent shows to keep the Gods amused.

THE PSYCHIC CIRCUS
Calling itself the Greatest Show in the Galaxy, the Psychic Circus travels from planet to planet. The Doctor turns the Gods' powers back on themselves, destroying them and blowing up the circus.

DATA FILE

HOMEWORLD:
SEGONAX

SPECIAL ABILITIES:
PSYCHIC POWER, ABLE TO EXIST IN TWO TIME ZONES

DOCTORS MET:
7TH

The Gods exist in two different dimensions. In their true time, they are living stone statues. On Segonax, the three Gods look like a mother and father with their small daughter.

GRACE HOLLOWAY
CLEVER COMPANION

A witty and intelligent heart surgeon, Grace helped the Eighth Doctor defeat the Master on the eve of the new millennium. The Master had opened the Eye of Harmony, the TARDIS's dangerous power source, in an attempt to steal the Doctor's lives, but Grace succeeded in jump-starting the ship before the Eye could destroy Earth.

REGENERATION
Grace operates on the fatally injured Seventh Doctor, not realising he has two hearts. He appears to die in theatre, but later regenerates as the Eighth Doctor. Grace drives the Doctor to her house for safety.

ALL CHANGE
The newly-regenerated Doctor returns to the TARDIS with Grace, only to face the power of his bitter enemy, the Master.

DATA FILE

ORIGIN:
SAN FRANCISCO, USA

OCCUPATION:
CARDIOLOGIST

DOCTORS MET:
7TH, 8TH

It took a while for Grace to believe the eccentric Eighth Doctor was really an alien from another planet. Even though they became close, Grace decided she couldn't face travelling in the TARDIS and decided to stay on Earth.

GRAYLE
AMERICAN CRIME BOSS

Julius Grayle is a powerful and wealthy crime magnate who lives in 1930s New York. Private investigator Garner describes him as the scariest guy he knows. Yet Grayle lives in fear of the mysterious Weeping Angels, with bars on the windows and locks on the doors of his mansion.

Grayle is a collector. His house is packed with priceless artefacts. But the jewel of his collection is a captured Weeping Angel, which he keeps chained up behind a curtain in his study.

A DANGEROUS OBSESSION
The Weeping Angels have fascinated Grayle all his life. He is obsessed with discovering what they are. He sends Garner to find out where they live, but the private investigator never returns.

ANGEL'S GRIP
Grayle has River Song from the Angel Detective Agency captured because he craves information about the Angels. His Angel prisoner grips her tightly and River breaks her own wrist as she escapes.

DATA FILE
ORIGIN:
NEW YORK, USA
SPECIAL ABILITIES:
CRUEL MANIPULATIONS
DOCTORS MET:
11TH

HAEMOVORES

VAMPIRE MUTATIONS

Haemovores were once human. These creatures are dependent on blood and live in water. At first their appearance is not unlike vampires, with pale skin and sharp claws, but eventually they turn into hideous mutations. Fenric, an ancient evil, uses them to aid his escape from the Doctor's trap.

DATA FILE

ORIGIN:
EARTH

SPECIAL ABILITIES:
INFECTING OTHERS

DOCTORS MET:
7TH

HAEMOVORE ARMY

Fenric transports the Ancient One, the last surviving creature on an alternative future Earth, back in time to free him at the right moment and create an army of Haemovores to serve him.

The first Haemovores were created by the Ancient One. Since Viking times, many humans have been infected and turned into these monsters that wait patiently until the time is right for Fenric's escape.

HANDBOTS
AUTOMATED MEDICAL ROBOTS

The Handbots look after sufferers of the deadly Chen7 virus in the Two Streams Facility on Apalapucia. Slow-moving and of limited intelligence, the blank-faced robots use their hands to "see" where they are going, and carry hypodermic needles and darts for administering medicine.

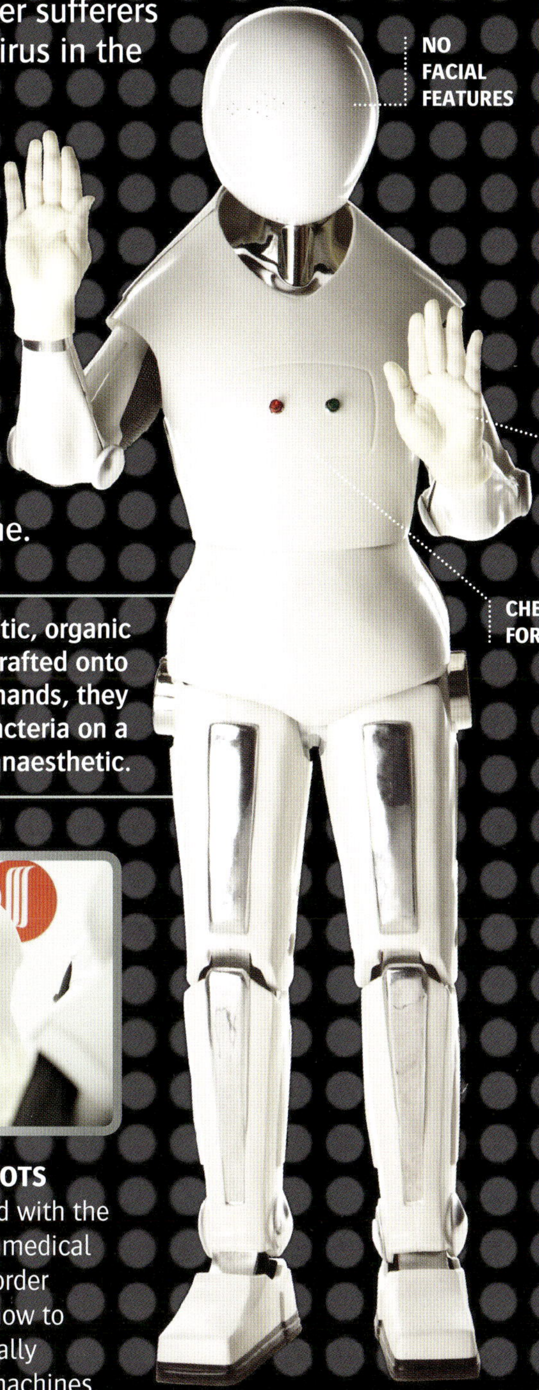

DATA FILE

HOMEWORLD: APALAPUCIA

SPECIAL ABILITIES: DELIVERING ANAESTHETIC BY TOUCH

DOCTORS MET: 11TH

Handbots have synthetic, organic skin which has been grafted onto their hands. Using their hands, they can even see types of bacteria on a person and administer anaesthetic.

BATTLE WITH THE HANDBOTS
When Amy becomes trapped with the Handbots, she realises their medical injections could kill her. In order to survive she has to learn how to reprogramme, and occasionally destroy, the well-meaning machines.

RORYBOT
Alone for many years, Amy ended up keeping one of the Handbots for company. She literally disarmed it by chopping off its hands, and drew a smiley face on its head. She even gave her robot pet a name – Rory!

HARRIET JONES

FORMER UK PRIME MINISTER

Harriet Jones is a quirky MP who meets the Doctor during the Slitheen's attempt to cause a nuclear war. Thanks to her role in defeating the aliens, Harriet is made Prime Minister. However, a furious Doctor later brings about her political downfall as punishment for her decision to destroy a retreating Sycorax spaceship.

INTELLIGENT AND MODEST

SMART OUTFIT AS BEFITS POLITICIAN

DEFYING THE DALEKS

Following a Dalek invasion, Harriet uses her sub-wave network to bring the Doctor's friends together in an attempt to reach the Time Lord. Tragically, the Daleks detect her signal and exterminate her!

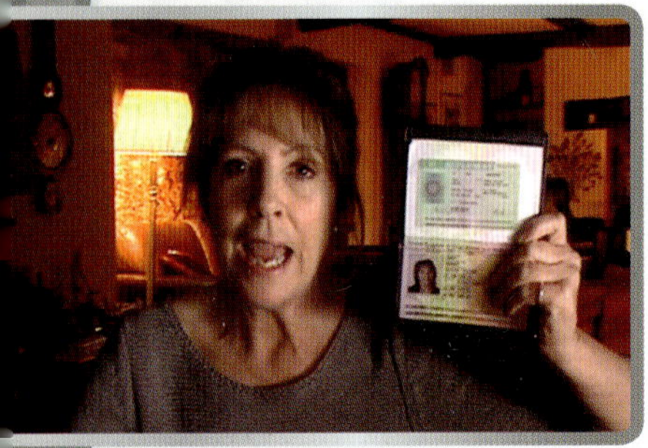

PASS PLEASE

Harriet always assumes no-one has heard of her. She introduces herself with a flash of her ID card, prompting the inevitable response, "We know who you are" – even from the Daleks and Sycorax!

Harriet is not afraid to make difficult decisions. She orders the Doctor to organise a missile strike that will destroy all the Slitheen invaders – and at great risk to herself.

DATA FILE

ORIGIN:
ENGLAND, EARTH

OCCUPATION:
MP FOR FLYDALE NORTH, UK PRIME MINISTER

DOCTORS MET:
9TH, 10TH

HARRY SULLIVAN
CLUMSY COMPANION

Brave, if a little old-fashioned, Harry Sullivan is a medical officer at UNIT who does his best to look after an erratic Doctor following his third regeneration. Once the Doctor has recovered, Harry ends up joining him aboard the TARDIS. The Doctor often becomes exasperated by the young man's clumsiness.

CLUMSY AND UNSUBTLE

SMART BLAZER

GET READY
The Fourth Doctor and his companions sometimes travel by transmat (matter transmitter) as well as by TARDIS. It doesn't always get them to where they want to go!

DATA FILE

ORIGIN:
ENGLAND, EARTH

OCCUPATION:
ROYAL NAVY SURGEON LIEUTENANT

DOCTORS MET:
4TH

SEEING DOUBLE
When the shape-shifting Zygons capture Harry, they use his body print to enable them to copy his form. Some time later, the Kraals make their own android duplicate of him!

Harry encounters some of the Doctor's most notorious enemies during his short time in the TARDIS. He meets a Sontaran on a ravaged Earth, battles the Cybermen on Voga, and even witnesses the birth of the Daleks on Skaro!

HATH
AMPHIBIOUS HUMANOIDS

The Doctor meets the fish-like Hath on the colony planet of Messaline. Once allies of the human settlers, the Hath initially helped them adapt the planet so that both races could establish a new society. Sadly, a war broke out and both sides used special progenation machines to replace their massacred troops.

In order to breathe properly, the Hath wear special masks filled with a form of liquid. This has the unfortunate effect of distorting their speech, and the resulting bubbling and gurgling noises make the creatures difficult to understand!

HATH HERO
After being captured by the Hath, Martha befriends one of their troops, Peck. He manages to save her from drowning in a swamp, but tragically loses his own life in the process.

DATA FILE

HOMEWORLD:
UNKNOWN

SPECIAL ABILITIES:
CONSIDERABLE STRENGTH AND STAMINA

DOCTORS MET:
10TH

HEADLESS MONKS

WARRIOR MONKS

The Headless Monks belong to a religious order who cut off their heads for their faith. Applicants are selected from visiting armies. Although headless, they are skilled warriors, and if they think anyone is trying to look under their hoods they will kill on the spot.

DATA FILE

HOMEWORLD: UNKNOWN

SPECIAL ABILITIES: COMBAT-TRAINED, ARMED WITH ELECTRICITY AND SWORDS

DOCTORS MET: 11TH

HUNGRY SKULLS

The skulls of the monks are stored in the Seventh Transept, a catacomb under their temple. The skulls eat rats and intruders.

UNDER THE HOOD

It is a Level One Heresy punishable by death to look under a Headless Monk's hood. Colonel Manton is granted special permission from the Papal Mainframe to unhood them in a public ceremony. It isn't pretty!

The Headless Monks form an uneasy alliance with the Clerics and Madame Kovarian in order to capture the pregnant Amy Pond and baby Melody. The Doctor disguises himself as one of the Headless order and infiltrates Demon's Run to save them.

HENRY AVERY
17TH CENTURY PIRATE CAPTAIN

Henry Avery was a respected naval officer who turned to piracy because of his greed for gold. The Doctor arrives on Avery's ship, *Fancy*, when it becomes the target of the mysterious Siren. Despite their misunderstandings, the Doctor comes to respect Avery and even calls on him for help on another occasion.

DATA FILE
ORIGIN: EARTH
INTERESTS: SAILING AND SWASHBUCKLING
DOCTORS MET: 11TH

An obsession with stealing treasure keeps Avery at sea, away from his wife and son Toby for three years. He promises to return but doesn't keep his word, so Toby stows away on his father's ship.

PLANK WALK
Avery is very suspicious of the Doctor. He refuses to believe the Doctor's TARDIS is a proper ship, thinks he is a stowaway and forces him to walk the plank.

THE SIREN
Avery discovers his crew are being held in stasis on the Siren's spaceship. They think the Siren is a sea monster, but she turns out to be a virtual doctor, who is programmed to heal sick people.

HENRY VAN STATTEN
ARROGANT AMERICAN BILLIONAIRE

Henry Van Statten is a powerful businessman who owns the internet and a secret museum full of alien artefacts. For years he has profited from alien technology that has fallen to Earth. He keeps a Dalek as a pet in his dungeon, completely unaware of how dangerous it is!

DATA FILE
ORIGIN:
EARTH
INTERESTS:
MAKING MONEY, COMPUTER PROGRAMMING, WIPING MINDS
DOCTORS MET:
9TH

METALTRON
The prize of Henry's collection is the "Metaltron" – a battle-scarred Dalek. He arrogantly thinks it will never escape its cage. But one touch from Rose Tyler frees it and it goes on a rampage.

Henry has agents around the world looking to recruit geniuses for his company. But he often fires them on a whim and wipes their memories. Even the president is at his mercy!

ALIEN MUSEUM
Van Statten has spent a fortune on his collection, which contains moondust, meteorites, parts of the Roswell spaceship, a stuffed Slitheen arm and a Cyberman's head.

IAN CHESTERTON
COMPETENT COMPANION

Like his fellow teacher, Barbara Wright, Ian Chesterton stumbles aboard the TARDIS one night, unaware of the incredible adventures to come. Honest and loyal, Ian is a practical man and his logical mind helps him escape numerous dangers. He is also not afraid of standing up to the cantankerous First Doctor!

SIR IAN OF JAFFA
One of the highlights of Ian's travels is when he is knighted by Richard the Lionheart. The King sends Ian as his emissary in search of the kidnapped Barbara.

Although he enjoys his travels in the TARDIS, Ian always longs to return to his own time. Both he and Barbara risk their lives to travel back to 1960s London using one of the Daleks' time machines.

DATA FILE

ORIGIN:
LONDON, ENGLAND

OCCUPATION:
SCIENCE TEACHER

DOCTORS MET:
1ST

ICE WARRIORS
MARTIAN CREATURES

Originally from the red planet Mars, the Ice Warriors are a powerful warrior race of reptilian humanoids. They have attempted to invade Earth on several occasions, wanting to transform its atmosphere into one more suitable to their biology.

DATA FILE

HOMEWORLD:
MARS

SPECIAL ABILITIES:
STRENGTH, SONIC WEAPONRY

DOCTORS MET:
2nd, 3rd

The Ice Warriors' greatest weakness is heat, which can leave them gasping for breath until they eventually die. Most of their large body is armour that protects the creature inside.

GALACTIC FEDERATION

Originally violent and extremely dangerous, the Ice Warriors decide to change their ways. They become peaceful and join the Galactic Federation.

FUTURE ICE AGE

During an Ice Age in Earth's future, an Ice Warrior is found frozen in a glacier. When it thaws out, the creature captures Victoria, the Doctor's companion. It wants her to help find the rest of its comrades who are still trapped inside the glacier.

IDRIS
HUMANOID HOST FOR THE TARDIS

Before Idris is filled with the soul, or Matrix, of the Doctor's TARDIS, she is a Patchwork Person who lives on a sentient asteroid, called House. Her only companions are two other Patchwork People and Nephew, a green-eyed Ood. Being possessed by the TARDIS makes Idris behave like she's mad – when the Doctor arrives, she bites him!

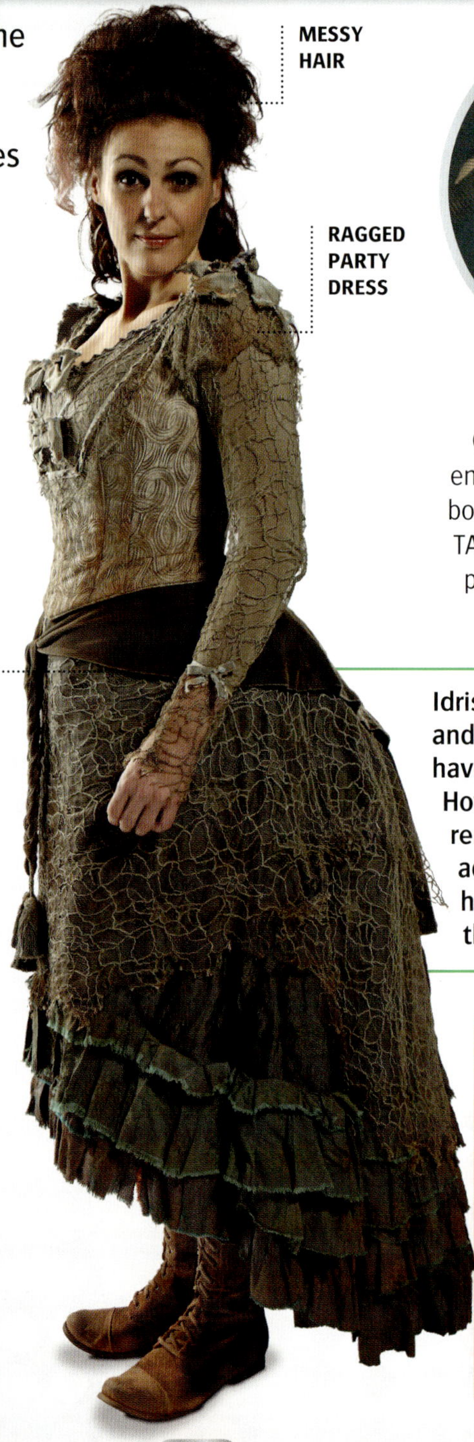

BRAIN DRAIN
On House's orders, Nephew empties Idris's mind from her body and then fills it with the TARDIS Matrix. It's extremely painful and her human body does not survive for long.

Idris often muddles tenses and talks about things that haven't happened yet. However, she clearly remembers all the adventures the TARDIS has shared with the Doctor.

JUNK TARDIS
When House steals the Doctor's TARDIS, Idris helps the Time Lord build a junk one to pursue him. She uses her power to energise it, but when the Matrix merges back with the TARDIS, Idris dies.

DATA FILE

HOMEWORLD:
HOUSE

SPECIAL ABILITIES:
HOST TO THE TARDIS MATRIX, SENDING TELEPATHIC MESSAGES

DOCTORS MET:
11TH

JABE

MEMBER OF A NOBLE TREE-PEOPLE

Three representatives from the Forest of Cheem arrive on board Platform One to witness the destruction of Earth. They are led by Jabe, a kind and flirtatious tree-woman who takes an instant liking to the Doctor. She does her best to console him when she discovers he is the last of his kind.

LUTE AND COFFA

Tree-forms Lute and Coffa are very loyal to Jabe. They are visibly distraught when the Ninth Doctor informs them of her death.

FAMILY TREE

Jabe offers the Doctor a cutting of her grandfather as a peace offering. She also reveals her reasons for coming to pay her respects to Earth, as a direct descendant of the planet's tropical rainforests.

DATA FILE

ORIGIN:
UNKNOWN

SPECIAL ABILITIES:
JABE COULD SHOOT A LIANA FROM HER WRIST

DOCTORS MET:
9TH

Jabe bravely helps the Doctor to re-activate Platform One's sun filters, but tragically dies when her wooden body catches fire in the space-station's ventilation chamber.

JACKIE TYLER
ROSE TYLER'S MOTHER

Hairdresser Jackie Tyler becomes a widow and single mum aged just 19. She lives with her daughter Rose in a council flat on the Powell Estate in London, until the Doctor arrives and turns their lives upside down. She is torn between wanting Rose to be happy and wanting to keep her safe.

DATA FILE
ORIGIN:
LONDON, EARTH
SPECIAL ABILITIES:
SLAPPING THE DOCTOR, PROTECTING HER DAUGHTER
DOCTORS MET:
9TH, 10TH

Rose is the most important thing in Jackie's life. She would do anything for her. When the Doctor whisks Rose away to see the universe, Jackie misses her terribly.

MIGHTY MUM
Jackie's adventures with the Doctor make her stronger and braver. When Rose crosses parallel worlds to find the Doctor, Jackie follows, determined to rescue her from the Daleks before returning to their new life in their alternative universe.

ALIEN FIGHTER
Jackie has witnessed Autons attacking London and was almost killed by a Slitheen. After a battle between Daleks and Cybermen, she becomes trapped in a parallel Earth alongside Rose.

JACKSON LAKE

VICTORIAN WOULD-BE DOCTOR

Jackson Lake is a brave and brash Victorian schoolteacher who becomes convinced he is an incarnation of the Doctor. With his faithful companion, Rosita, he constructs his own versions of the TARDIS (a hot-air balloon) and a not-so-sonic screwdriver! He also spends time investigating the presence of a group of Cybermen in 19th-century London.

DATA FILE

ORIGIN:
SUSSEX, ENGLAND

OCCUPATION:
MATHEMATICS TEACHER

DOCTORS MET:
10TH

MISTAKEN IDENTITY
When the Cybermen kill his wife and kidnap his son, Jackson wants to forget. He finds one of their infostamps – a steel data storage device – but it backfires and makes him believe he is the Doctor.

NICE TO MEET YOU
In a snowy street, the Tenth Doctor meets a man he thinks could be a future incarnation of himself. It's actually Jackson Lake, who believes he himself is the travelling Time Lord.

With the Doctor's help, Jackson recovers his painful memories and true identity. The two manage to defeat the Cybermen who have been building a huge CyberKing using child slaves. Courageous as ever, Jackson helps free the children, including his own son.

JAGRAFESS

EDITOR-IN-CHIEF OF SATELLITE FIVE

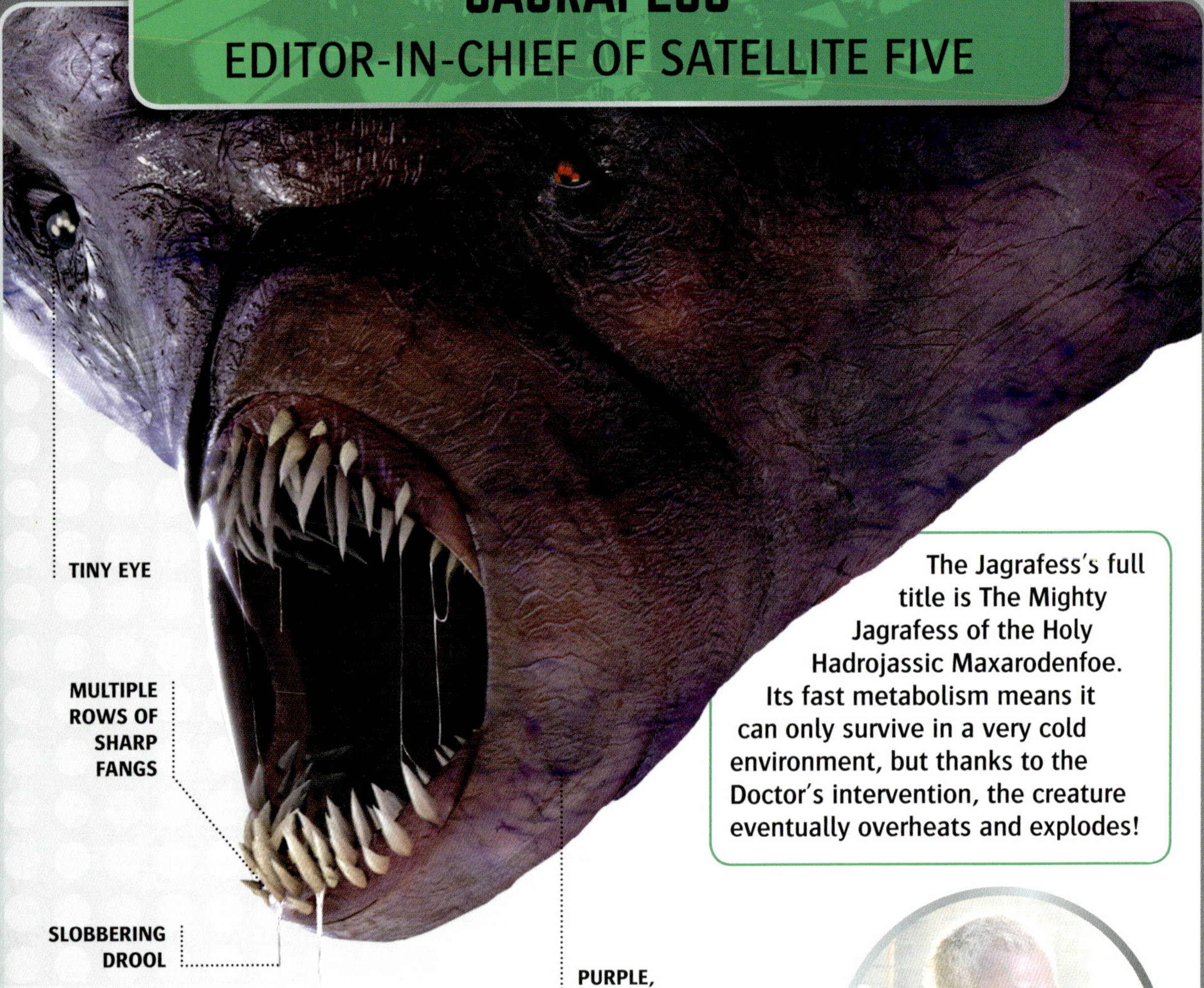

The Jagrafess's full title is The Mighty Jagrafess of the Holy Hadrojassic Maxarodenfoe. Its fast metabolism means it can only survive in a very cold environment, but thanks to the Doctor's intervention, the creature eventually overheats and explodes!

Resembling a massive slab of meat, the Jagrafess is a vicious, slimy creature which clings to the ceiling of Floor 500 aboard Satellite Five. Installed by the Daleks, it manipulates the news reports broadcast by the station and creates a climate of fear that enables it to control the whole of humanity.

DATA FILE

ORIGIN:
UNKNOWN

SPECIAL ABILITIES:
CAN LIVE UP TO 3,000 YEARS

DOCTORS MET:
9TH

PRISONERS OF THE JAGRAFESS

The Doctor and Rose are captured by the Jagrafess and interrogated by the Editor, its shifty employee. The Editor wants to use the Doctor's TARDIS to rewrite history and prevent humanity from ever developing.

JAMIE MCCRIMMON
FAITHFUL COMPANION

James "Jamie" Robert McCrimmon first met the Second Doctor in the aftermath of the infamous Battle of Culloden in 1746. While he isn't the brightest of the Doctor's companions, he is certainly one of the bravest and most loyal, and he travels with the Second Doctor for a long time.

When the Time Lords put the Doctor on trial, part of his punishment was the loss of his companions. Jamie returns to Scotland and the Time Lords wipe his memory so he can only recall his first adventure with the Doctor.

SHEEP'S WOOL SCARF

SCOTTISH KILT FROM THE HIGHLANDS

DATA FILE

ORIGIN:
HIGHLANDS OF SCOTLAND, EARTH

CHARACTER TRAITS:
LOYALTY

DOCTORS MET:
2ND, 6TH

WHITE FRIGHT

When the Doctor activates the TARDIS's emergency unit, the ship is taken out of time and space. Jamie, together with fellow companion Zoe, soon finds himself in a nightmarish void, surrounded by sinister white robots.

FIGHTING DALEKS

Although Jamie is astounded by many of the aliens he meets during his adventures, he isn't fazed by the Daleks. He bravely takes them on and even manages to destroy a couple!

JENNY
THE DOCTOR'S DAUGHTER

Jenny is a generation 5000 soldier created from the Doctor's DNA to fight the Hath on planet Messaline. She is a child of the Progenation Machine and was "born" fully-grown, primed to take orders and ready for combat. Donna Noble names her Jenny because she is a "generated anomaly".

TWO HEARTS LIKE THE DOCTOR

COMBAT-READY

MILITARY-STYLE BOOTS

BITTER WAR
The humans on Messaline are locked in war against the fish-faced Hath. Jenny is born with the knowledge that she must fight the Hath until the war is won.

Jenny and her father don't bond easily. Her natural instinct is to fight, whereas the Doctor wants peace. But their adventure on Messaline reveals how similar they both are.

DYING FOR THE DOCTOR
Jenny takes a bullet to protect the Doctor and dies in his arms. Later, energy from a terraforming device brings her back to life and she sets off to explore the universe.

DATA FILE

HOMEWORLD:
MESSALINE

SPECIAL ABILITIES:
FIGHTING, ACROBATICS, EXPLOSIVES

DOCTORS MET:
10TH

JO GRANT
CREATIVE COMPANION

A loveable scatterbrain, Jo Grant manages to wangle herself a job at UNIT as the Third Doctor's companion, thanks to her powerful uncle at the United Nations. At first the Doctor is horrified at the thought of having such a clumsy assistant around him, but he soon grows very fond of her.

JO JONES
Jo eventually leaves the Doctor after falling in love with Clifford Jones, a brilliant professor who wants to end world hunger, and who reminds Jo of a younger version of the Doctor.

ABLE TO RESIST HYPNOSIS ATTEMPTS

NATURALLY ENTHUSIASTIC

CROPPED, LACE-UP JACKET

Although she has a knack for putting her foot in it, Jo is always enthusiastic and often very resourceful. She is good at escapology and picking locks, and she even lists cryptology, safe-breaking and explosives amongst her repertoire of skills!

DATA FILE
ORIGIN:
ENGLAND, EARTH

OCCUPATION:
UNIT AGENT

DOCTORS MET:
3RD, 11TH

JOAN REDFERN
SCHOOL NURSE

Joan Redfern is a kind and helpful matron at Farringham School for Boys. After her husband dies in the Boer War, she falls for an unusual history teacher called John Smith. She has no idea that he is really the Doctor in a human disguise until the sinister Family of Blood hunt him down.

John Smith intrigues Joan. She is fascinated by his Journal of Impossible Things – a dream diary packed full of monsters and other worlds. She never imagines it might all be real.

COME WITH ME
After defeating the Family, the Doctor asks Joan to travel with him. However, she declines as she is unable to reconcile this man, bringing death and destruction in his wake, as being the same man she fell in love with.

1910 ERA PARTY DRESS

REALITY HURTS
Joan and John's blossoming relationship is cut short when the Family attacks the school during a village dance. Joan is heartbroken to realise the man she loves must sacrifice himself to return to his true identity as the Doctor.

DATA FILE
ORIGIN:
EARTH

SPECIAL ABILITIES:
NURSING, DANCING, BEING BRAVE

DOCTORS MET:
10TH

JOHN LUMIC
CREATOR OF THE CYBERMEN

Lumic is the owner of Cybus Industries on a parallel version of Earth. Wheelchair-bound and suffering from a terminal illness, he is desperate to prolong his own life and so he develops the ultimate upgrade for humanity. His grisly process involves removing a person's brain and placing it in a protective metal exoskeleton.

DATA FILE

HOMEWORLD:
PARALLEL EARTH

OCCUPATION:
OWNER OF CYBUS INDUSTRIES

DOCTORS MET:
10TH

CYBER CONVERSION
When Lumic's life-support systems are damaged, his Cybermen realise he is in pain and force him to undergo the upgrade process. Despite Lumic's objections, they convert him into their Cyber Controller.

BREATHING APPARATUS

Lumic believes his motives are for the good of mankind, reasoning that people would no longer have to suffer from disease or painful emotions. Fortunately, the Doctor manages to stop his insane plan, and Lumic's cyber-form is eventually destroyed.

JOHN RIDDELL
BIG-GAME HUNTER

John Riddell is a big-game hunter on the African plains, originating from early 20th century England. He is old friends with the Doctor and shares his love of fun and adventure. When a Silurian ark carrying dinosaurs hurtles on a crash-course with Earth, Riddell jumps at the chance to help the Doctor stop it.

THRILL-SEEKER
Nothing makes Riddell happier than being in danger! He finds the prospect of fighting Raptors and the strong likelihood of being blown up thrilling.

LIGHT KHAKI CAMOUFLAGE CLOTHING FOR HUNTING

SHEATHED HUNTING KNIFE

QUEEN NEFERTITI
At first, John Riddell and Queen Nefertiti find each other distinctly annoying, but they soon start flirting. And when Riddell returns to Africa, Neffy joins him.

DATA FILE

ORIGIN:
ENGLAND, EARTH

INTERESTS:
HUNTING, FIGHTING RAPTORS

DOCTORS MET:
11TH

Riddell has hunted big beasts all his life and has to fight his urge to kill all the space-bound dinosaurs. More than anything he wants a dinosaur tooth to take home!

JUDOON
INTERGALACTIC LAW ENFORCERS

Much like rhinoceroses, the huge and powerful Judoon are essentially police for hire. As well as being used to bring murderers to justice, they also provide security for the law-making Shadow Proclamation. They aren't known for their intelligence, though, and their predictable methods sometimes lead to mistakes.

DATA FILE

HOMEWORLD:
UNKNOWN

SPECIAL ABILITIES:
LARGE LUNGS CAN COPE WITH LOW LEVELS OF OXYGEN

DOCTORS MET:
10TH, 11TH

STOLEN HOSPITAL
Hired to eliminate a murdering alien Plasmavore, the Judoon search every floor of the Royal Hope Hospital – but not before they transport the entire building to the Moon, taking Martha Jones with it!

The Judoon possess impressive technology. They travel through space in massive, cylindrical spaceships and can surround buildings with powerful force shields. They use hand-held translator devices that analyse the speech of alien beings, allowing the Judoon to communicate freely.

K-9
ROBOT-DOG COMPANION

Once described by the Doctor as his "second best friend", K-9 is a brilliant super-computer with an endearing personality, even if he sometimes comes across as a bit of a know-it-all. The original K-9 was built in the year 5000 by dog-loving Professor Marius, who gave him to the Doctor as a gift.

DATA FILE

HOMEWORLD:
BI-AL FOUNDATION, ASTEROID K4067

SPECIAL ABILITIES:
ENCYCLOPEDIC MEMORY BANK, VAST INTELLIGENCE

DOCTORS MET:
4TH, 10TH

A PRESENT FOR SARAH JANE
When Sarah Jane met the Tenth Doctor, he was able to temporarily repair her broken K-9 Mk 3. He later built a fourth version for her, complete with two sonic lipsticks and a scanner watch.

K-9 is loyal and fearless, with large memory banks and highly sophisticated sensors. There have been four versions of K-9. Mk 1 stayed on Gallifrey with the Doctor's companion Leela, while Mk 2 was given to the Doctor's friend Romana. Mk 3 and Mk 4 belonged to Sarah Jane.

KAHLER-JEX
ALIEN DOCTOR

Kahler-Jex is a Kahler scientist who experiments on his own people in order to win a war. When one of his cyborg soldiers goes rogue and starts hunting down its makers, Jex flees to Earth. He hides in a town called Mercy where he becomes their doctor.

Jex considers himself to be a war hero, but he is also haunted by guilt. To atone for his crimes, he does his best to help the people of Mercy, saving them from cholera and giving them electricity.

THE WAR IS OVER
Knowing his old volunteer Tek will tear the universe apart in order to find him, Jex takes matters into his own hands and ends the war by blowing up his own spaceship.

LIVING A LIE
The Doctor normally loves the Kahler, calling them "one of the most ingenious races in the galaxy". But on discovering the truth about Jex, he is so horrified he drives him out of town.

DATA FILE
HOMEWORLD:
KAHLER
SPECIAL ABILITIES:
ADVANCED MEDICAL KNOWLEDGE
DOCTORS MET:
11TH

KAHLER-TEK

THE GUNSLINGER

Kahler-Tek was originally a volunteer who signed up for special training, only to be experimented on by Kahler scientist, Jex, who turned Tek into a cyborg assassin by fusing weaponry to his body. Tek and the other cyborg creations were then programmed to kill in order to bring an end to the nine-year war on Kahler.

DATA FILE

HOMEWORLD: KAHLER

SPECIAL ABILITIES: MASSIVE FIREPOWER, MILITARY STRATEGIES, SHORT-RANGE TELEPORTATION

DOCTORS MET: 11TH

Jex's cyborgs are so deadly they soon end the war on Kahler. Aware that he has become a monster, Tek seeks revenge on his creators, for himself and his colleagues killed or disfigured at Jex's hands. Tek pursues Jex to the town of Mercy, where he is nicknamed The Gunslinger.

A NEW MARSHAL

Once Jex has been dealt with, Kahler-Tek decides to go into the desert and self-destruct. However, the Doctor persuades him to become protector and marshal of Mercy.

KAMELION
ROBOTIC COMPANION

Kamelion is a shape-changing android originally used by invaders of the planet Xeriphas. When the Master discovers the robot, he uses it to impersonate King John of England with the intention of changing the course of history. The Doctor succeeds in foiling his plan and Kamelion joins him in the TARDIS.

DATA FILE

HOMEWORLD:
UNKNOWN

SPECIAL ABILITIES:
SHAPE-CHANGING

DOCTORS MET:
5TH

MASTER MIND

The Master later manages to regain control of Kamelion. The Time Lord had accidentally shrunk himself and needed the android's help to return him to full size!

With Kamelion under the Master's mental control, the Doctor is forced to attack it. He reluctantly induces a reaction in its psycho-circuits – the electronic equivalent of a heart attack. He then uses the Master's own weapon to destroy the damaged robot.

MUSIC MAESTRO

Kamelion is a complex mass of artificial neurons, capable of infinite form. He is controlled by simple concentration and psychokinetics – and can even be made to play musical instruments!

KATARINA
TROJAN COMPANION

A gentle handmaiden to High Priestess Cassandra, Katarina of Troy meets the Doctor when he visits the besieged city in 1184 BC. She joins the TARDIS crew after helping the Doctor's injured companion Steven Taylor inside the ship. With no knowledge of technology, Katarina believes the TARDIS to be the Doctor's temple.

SELF SACRIFICE
When a crazed criminal tries to blackmail the Doctor by taking Katarina hostage, she saves her friends by opening an airlock door, sending both her and the convict into space.

After entering the TARDIS, Katarina tells the Doctor that she knows she will die. She believes he is Zeus and is taking her to the Place of Perfection. Following her tragic death, a shaken Doctor hopes Katarina has found such a place.

DATA FILE
ORIGIN:
TROY, EARTH
OCCUPATION:
HANDMAIDEN
DOCTORS MET:
1ST

KATE STEWART
THE BRIGADIER'S DAUGHTER

Kate Stewart is head of Scientific Research at UNIT. Although it is unusual for a scientist to run the military organisation, strong-minded Kate drags UNIT kicking and screaming into the 21st century. She successfully leads the investigation when millions of mysterious cubes suddenly appear across the globe.

DOESN'T WEAR UNIT UNIFORM

TEAM CUBE
Kate enlists the Doctor's help to figure out what the cubes are and who sent them. She is delighted to have the opportunity to work with her father's old friend.

DON'T DESPAIR
The sheer scale of the Shakri's cube attack initially causes Kate to despair. But with some encouraging words from the Doctor, her leadership qualities shine through.

DATA FILE
ORIGIN:
EARTH

SPECIAL ABILITIES:
LEADERSHIP, INTELLIGENCE, INITIATIVE

DOCTORS MET:
11TH

Depite being the daughter of former UNIT Commander Brigadier Lethbridge-Stewart, Kate is determined to make her own way in the world. She drops the "Lethbridge" from her name in order to avoid rumours of favouritism.

KAZRAN SARDICK
MISERABLE MISER

Kazran Sardick is a wealthy money-lender who controls the skies of Sardicktown. But years of being on his own have twisted him into a mean old man, just like his father had been. The Doctor travels into Kazran's past to force him to change his cruel ways.

Kazran is cruel – he refuses to help a spaceship trapped in the cloud belt carrying 4,000 people. Like his father before him, Kazran freezes the relatives of people he loans money to and allows fierce Fog Sharks to frighten the Sardicktown citizens – thus maintaining his control over them.

FIRST LOVE

As a twelve-year-old boy, Kazran befriends a woman called Abigail Pettigrew. She is kept locked up in a cryo-cylinder in Kazran's father's basement. Every Christmas eve, Kazran and the Doctor visit Abigail and they all go on adventures together in the TARDIS.

CHRISTMAS DAY

When the older Kazran finally sees the error of his ways, he releases Abigail from the frozen chamber so they can spend one last day together.

DATA FILE

HOMEWORLD:
EMBER

SPECIAL ABILITIES:
CONTROLLING THE FOG LAYER, ISOMETRIC CONTROLS

DOCTORS MET:
11TH

KRILLITANES
COMPOSITE ALIEN SPECIES

DATA FILE
HOMEWORLD:
UNKNOWN
SPECIAL ABILITIES:
EVOLVING ANATOMY
DOCTORS MET:
10TH

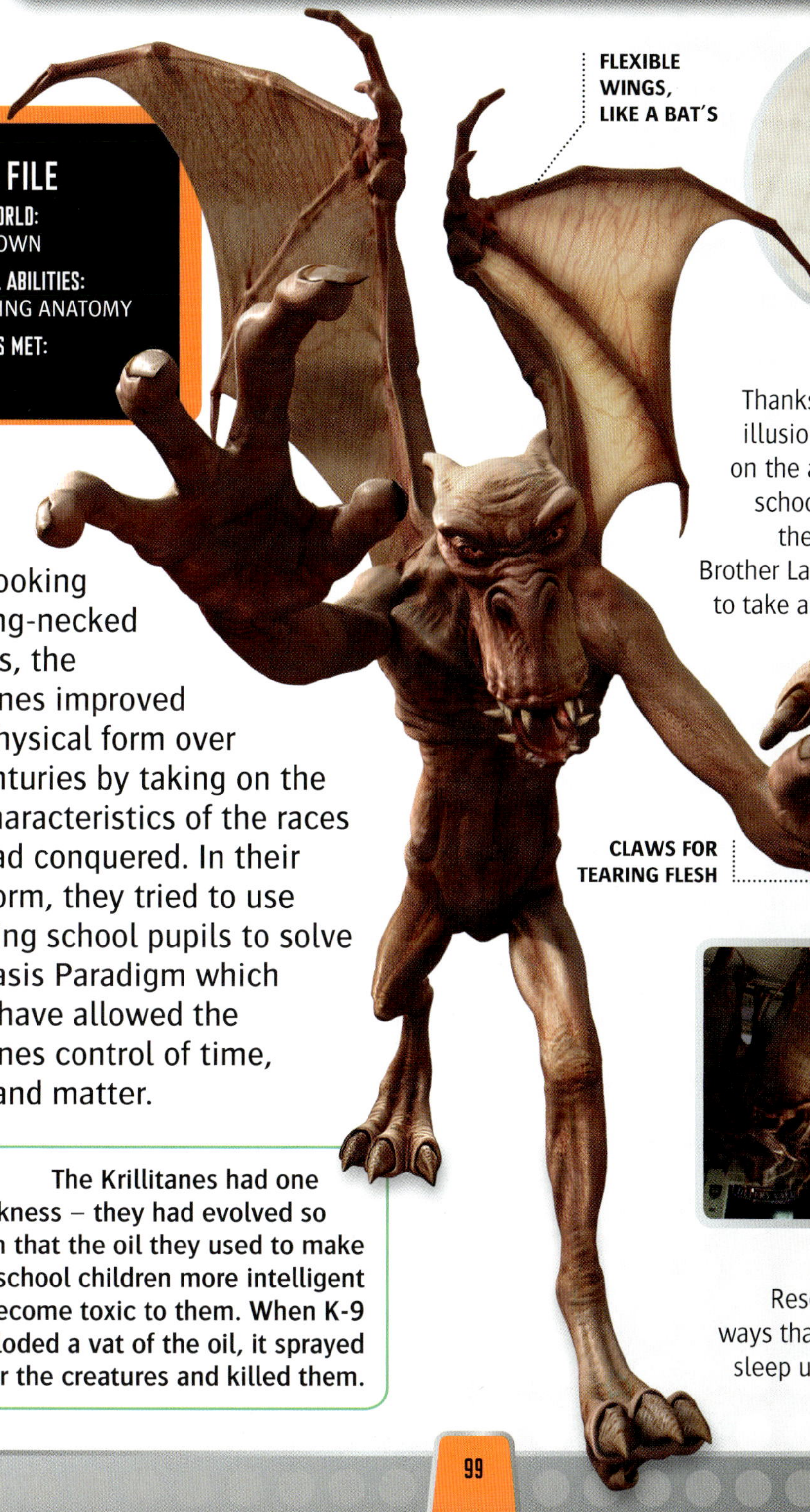

ALIEN TEACHERS
Thanks to a simple morphic illusion, the Krillitanes take on the appearance of human schoolteachers to disguise themselves. Their leader Brother Lassar, however, prefers to take an actual human form.

Once looking like long-necked humans, the Krillitanes improved their physical form over the centuries by taking on the best characteristics of the races they had conquered. In their alien form, they tried to use unwitting school pupils to solve the Skasis Paradigm which would have allowed the Krillitanes control of time, space and matter.

The Krillitanes had one weakness – they had evolved so much that the oil they used to make the school children more intelligent had become toxic to them. When K-9 exploded a vat of the oil, it sprayed over the creatures and killed them.

BAT BEDROOM
Resembling bats in more ways than one, the Krillitanes sleep upside down and have acute hearing.

KROTONS

CRYSTALLINE LIFE FORMS

Bulky and somewhat clumsy life forms, a group of angry Krotons are found in suspended animation on a planet inhabited by Gonds, a near-human race. After the Krotons' spaceship had crash-landed there, the Krotons set about educating and ruling the Gonds.

TARDIS ATTACK

One Kroton tries to destroy the TARDIS and thinks it succeeds. However, the Doctor had remembered to set the Hostile Action Displacement System controls – and the TARDIS dematerialises to safety.

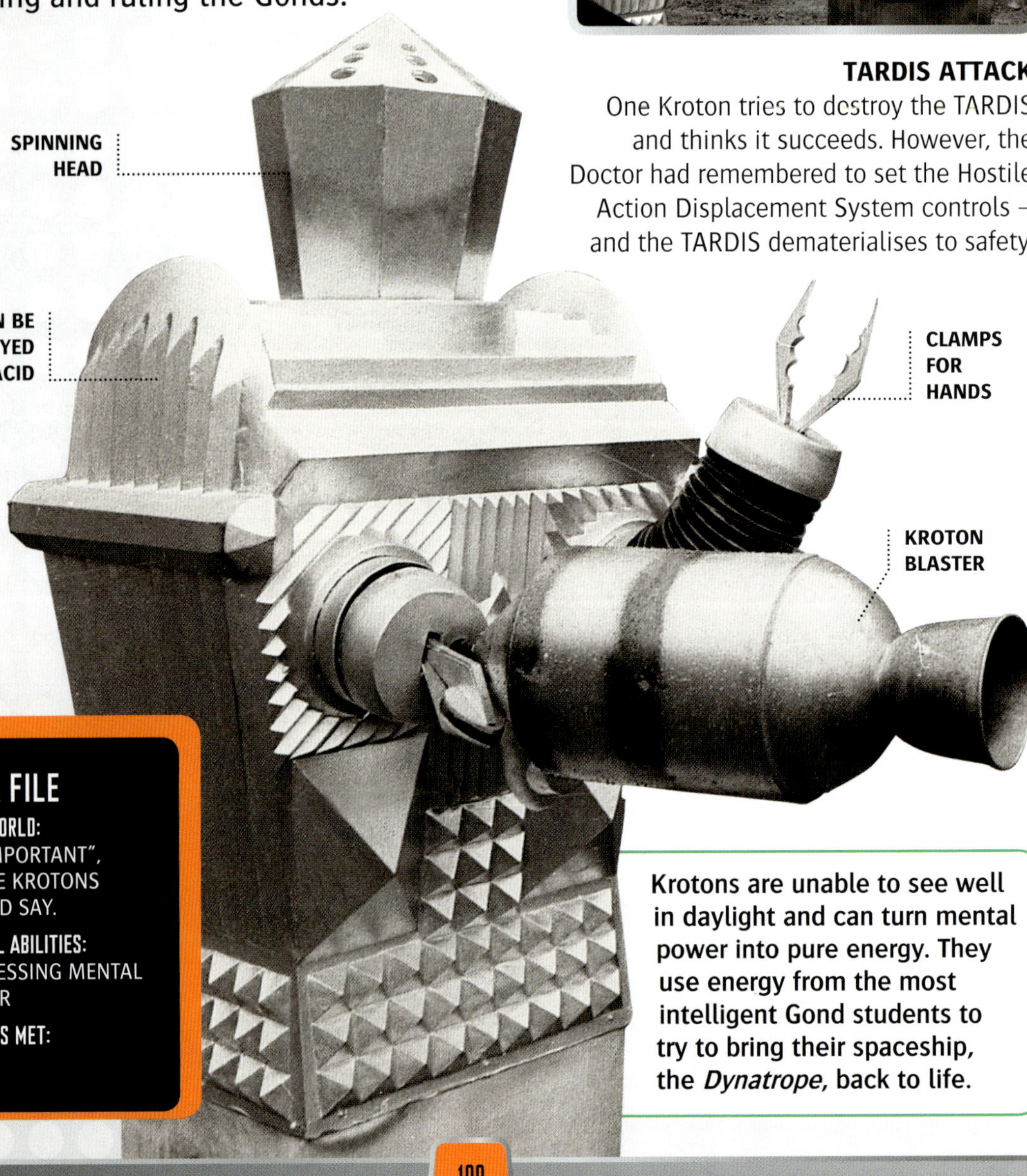

DATA FILE

HOMEWORLD: "UNIMPORTANT", AS THE KROTONS WOULD SAY.

SPECIAL ABILITIES: HARNESSING MENTAL POWER

DOCTORS MET: 2ND

Krotons are unable to see well in daylight and can turn mental power into pure energy. They use energy from the most intelligent Gond students to try to bring their spaceship, the *Dynatrope*, back to life.

KRYNOIDS

HOSTILE ALIEN WEEDS

These monsters are deadly, carnivorous alien plant creatures. The bulky, green form can expand incredibly quickly and is also able to control other plants in close proximity. Contact with Krynoids is fatal to human beings.

Two Krynoid pods are found buried in Antarctic permafrost. One pod reacts to ultraviolet radiation and turns a scientist into a Krynoid creature. A second pod is stolen and taken to the UK – nearly destroying all human life.

DESTRUCTION PLAN

The stolen Krynoid pod rapidly expands in size, and is soon the size of a house. It terrorises the Doctor and Sarah Jane, and is eventually blown up by an RAF squadron.

DATA FILE

HOMEWORLD:
UNKNOWN

SPECIAL ABILITIES:
RAPID GROWTH, PSYCHIC, UNAFFECTED BY EXTREME HEAT AND COLD

DOCTORS MET:
4TH

LADY CASSANDRA O'BRIEN

SELF-PROCLAIMED LAST HUMAN

Lady Cassandra is one of the guests aboard Platform One come to observe the Earth's destruction. Vain, selfish and money-grabbing, she describes herself as the "last pure human" alive. However, all that is left of her is a piece of tightly stretched skin, thanks to the 708 surgical operations Cassandra has had to extend her life.

DATA FILE

ORIGIN:
LOS ANGELES CREVASSE, EARTH

SPECIAL ABILITIES:
STAYING ALIVE WITHOUT A BODY

DOCTORS MET:
9TH, 10TH

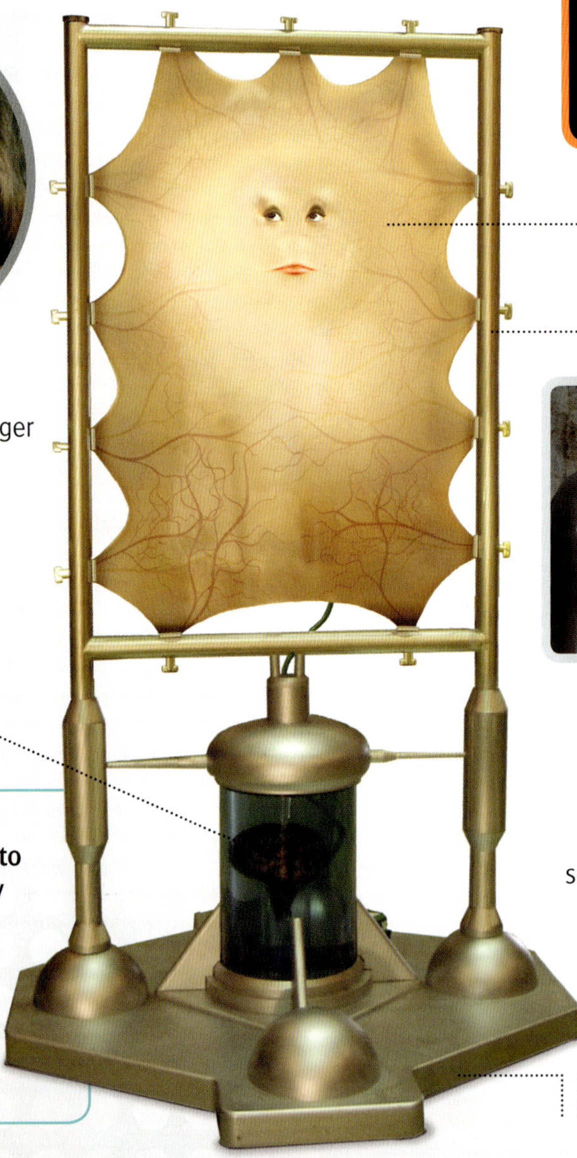

WHAT A NAME!
When Cassandra was younger she was considered to be very beautiful. Her full name is Lady Cassandra O'Brien.Δ17 (pronounced Dot Delta Seventeen).

In her stretched state, Cassandra's skin needs to be moisturised regularly to stop it drying out. When her first piece of skin rips, she simply replaces it with another piece taken from the back of her body!

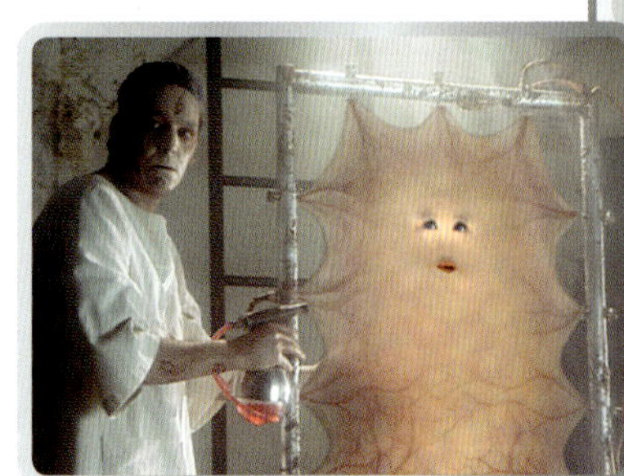

CASSANDRA'S DEATH
Fed up of being flat, Cassandra tries to find herself a new body. She takes over her devoted servant Chip, but his weak body can't cope and Cassandra finally dies.

LADY CHRISTINA DE SOUZA
PROFESSIONAL THIEF

Cheeky and charming, Christina is an aristocrat who gets her kicks from stealing precious artefacts, including the priceless Cup of Athelstan. She tries to escape on a London bus which takes her on the greatest adventure of her life – travelling through a wormhole to the ravaged planet of San Helios.

EXCELLENT EYESIGHT AND QUICK WITS

FITTED CLOTHES FOR NIMBLE ACROBATICS

BLACK CLOTHES GO UNSEEN IN THE DARK

RUBBER-SOLED BOOTS REDUCE SOUND OF FOOTSTEPS

CLEVER CAT
When she stole the gold Cup of Athelstan from the International Gallery, Christina left a Japanese waving cat statue as her calling card.

DATA FILE
ORIGIN:
ENGLAND, EARTH
SPECIAL ABILITIES:
CAT BURGLARY
DOCTORS MET:
10TH

FLYING BUS
Christina's skills as a cat burglar helped her penetrate a crashed spaceship to recover its anti-gravity clamps. The Doctor then used the devices to fly the battered bus back to Earth!

Christina loves her exciting escapade with the Doctor and is eager to join him in the TARDIS. However, the Doctor refuses as he has lost too many companions, and Christina ends up flying away in the bus, heading off on her own adventures.

LEELA
CURIOUS COMPANION

Leela is a warrior of the Sevateem, a tribe of humans on an alien world which has regressed to the point of savagery. Although uneducated and ignorant of technology, Leela is bright and inquisitive and tends to learn quickly. The Fourth Doctor does his best to educate her and attempts to curb her violent tendencies.

PRIMITIVE ANIMAL SKIN OUTFIT

CHUNKY CROSSBOW

DATA FILE

ORIGIN: UNNAMED ALIEN WORLD

OCCUPATION: WARRIOR

DOCTORS MET: 4TH

Leela is a creature of instinct and can often tell if danger is nearby. Much to the Doctor's annoyance, she is also familiar with a number of weapons, including hunting knives, crossbows and poisonous darts called Janis thorns.

RAT ATTACK
Although handy in a fight, Leela is helpless against a savage sewer rat that had been made many times larger, thanks to the experiments of war criminal Magnus Greel. She narrowly manages to escape.

LIZ SHAW
STUDIOUS COMPANION

Doctor Elizabeth Shaw is a distinguished Cambridge scientist. She was drafted in by the Brigadier to become UNIT's scientific advisor, despite her initial scepticism about the existence of aliens. When the Doctor is exiled to Earth, Liz's role quickly changes to that of companion as she ends up assisting him on his investigations.

PARALLEL LIZ
The Doctor has a nasty shock when he accidentally travels to a parallel world and meets Section Leader Shaw – a much stricter and more severe version of his friend.

Liz is one of the Third Doctor's most resourceful and intelligent companions. An expert in meteorites, she has degrees in various subjects, including medicine and physics. She eventually decides to leave UNIT and return to her own research at Cambridge.

DATA FILE

ORIGIN:
ENGLAND, EARTH

OCCUPATION:
SCIENTIST

DOCTORS MET:
3RD

LIZ TEN
RULER OF *STARSHIP UK*

Otherwise known as Queen Elizabeth the Tenth, Liz Ten is the ruler of *Starship UK*, a ship that saved her people from devastating solar flares. Cool and collected, she believes her government is hiding a dark secret and is determined to find out how *Starship UK* could appear to fly without engines.

STARSHIP SECRET
Liz is horrified when she discovers she has been keeping secrets from herself. She is conditoned to find out every 10 years that the *Starship UK* has been built around a tortured star whale and has repeatedly chosen to forget the painful truth.

Liz Ten believes she is 50 and she has ruled for 10 years. However, the Doctor deduces that her government has slowed down her body clock. She is actually about 300 years old.

ROYAL IDENTITY
In order to carry out her investigations in secret, Liz Ten wears a porcelain mask perfectly sculpted to her facial features. However, she doesn't realise that the mask is hundreds of years old.

DATA FILE
ORIGIN:
EARTH

OCCUPATION:
RULER OF *STARSHIP UK*

DOCTORS MET:
11TH

MACRA
GIANT CRAB CREATURES

Enormous crustaceans, the Macra live in the enclosed Undercity of New New York where they feed on the poisonous exhaust fumes of thousands of gridlocked vehicles. Once intelligent and manipulative creatures, the Macra have devolved over billions of years to become mindless beasts, albeit with a strong instinct for survival.

The Doctor met an earlier form of Macra on a human colony world, a long time before they eventually devolved. These creatures also fed on gas and brainwashed the inhabitants into mining it for them.

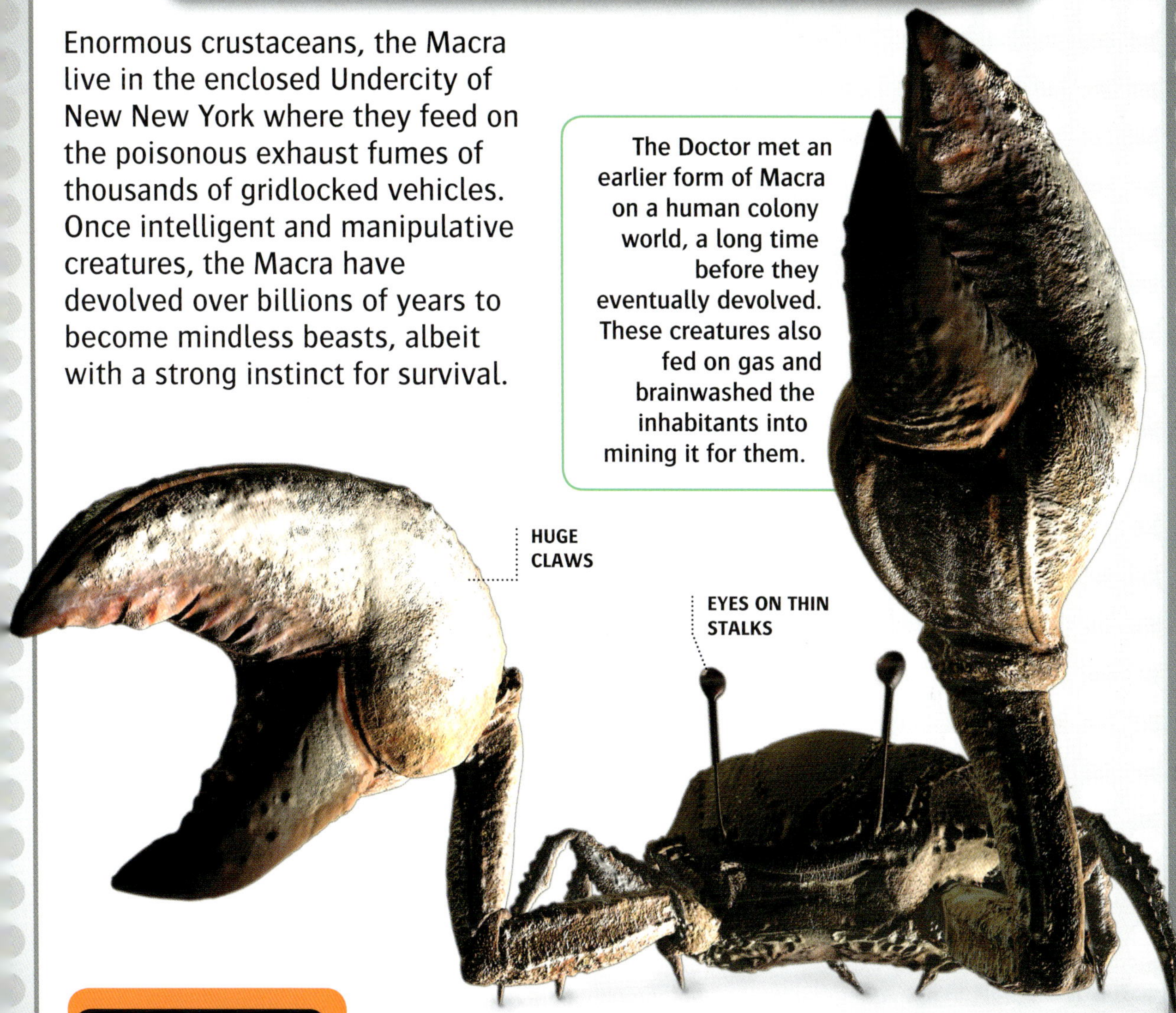

DATA FILE

ORIGIN:
UNKNOWN

SPECIAL ABILITIES:
CAN BREATHE TOXIC GAS

DOCTOR MET:
2ND, 10TH

MACRA ATTACK

When the Doctor's companion Martha is kidnapped and taken to the low-level fast lane, the car she is travelling in is attacked by the Macra, who instinctively protect their territory.

MADAME DE POMPADOUR
THE GIRL IN THE FIREPLACE

Madame de Pompadour, known as Reinette, is the mistress of King Louis XV. At the age of seven, she discovered a deadly Clockwork Robot under her bed, but, luckily, is saved by the Doctor. Reinette's bedroom fireplace contains a portal between a 51st-century damaged spaceship and 18th-century Paris.

ALSO KNOWN AS JEANNE ANTOINETTE POISSON

EMBROIDERED 18TH-CENTURY DRESS

TIMELESS LOVE

Time passes at different speeds for the Doctor and Reinette. A minute for him is years for her. He watches over Reinette her entire life. In turn, Reinette falls in love with her "Fireplace Man".

BRAIN ACHE

When Reinette turns 37, the Clockwork Robots believe her brain can be used to fix their ship and return to take it. Even in danger, Reinette never doubts the Doctor will save her.

Reinette becomes involved with the Clockwork Robots because their spaceship, the *SS Madame de Pompadour*, and Reinette share the same name.

DATA FILE

ORIGIN:
EARTH

OCCUPATION:
ACCOMPLISHED ACTRESS, ARTIST, MUSICIAN AND DANCER

DOCTORS MET:
10TH

MADAME KOVARIAN

HUMANOID ENVOY OF THE SILENCE

This wicked woman serves the religious order known as the Silence. She is charged with creating a weapon to kill the Doctor so that he never reaches the fields of Trenzalore, where "Silence will fall". That weapon is Melody Pond – Amy and Rory's part-Time Lord child, whom Kovarian raises to be a psychopath.

EYE DRIVE

DATA FILE

HOMEWORLD: UNKNOWN

INTERESTS: TRICKING THE DOCTOR

DOCTORS MET: 11TH

Madame Kovarian trains Melody for a single purpose – to kill the Doctor. When Melody regenerates into River Song, Madame Kovarian forces her to shoot the Doctor at Lake Silencio.

TRICKED TWICE

Madame Kovarian uses trickery to get her own way. She kidnaps Amy so she can watch over her whilst she is pregnant – fooling even the Doctor by leaving a Ganger in her place. Then, when Melody is born, she swaps the baby for another Ganger, much to the unsuspecting Amy's dismay.

HIGH-HEELS MAKE HER FEEL MORE POWERFUL

TERMINATED

Like all servants of the Silence, Madame Kovarian wears an Eye Drive so that she remembers their existence. She is horrified when the Silence use it to electrocute her.

MADAME VASTRA
SILURIAN SWORDFIGHTER

Madame Vastra is a Silurian warrior who lives in Victorian England with her human wife Jenny. She is a skilled swordfighter who puts her superior intelligence to good use by working for Scotland Yard. She helps them crack cases, hunts down criminals and eats them for dinner!

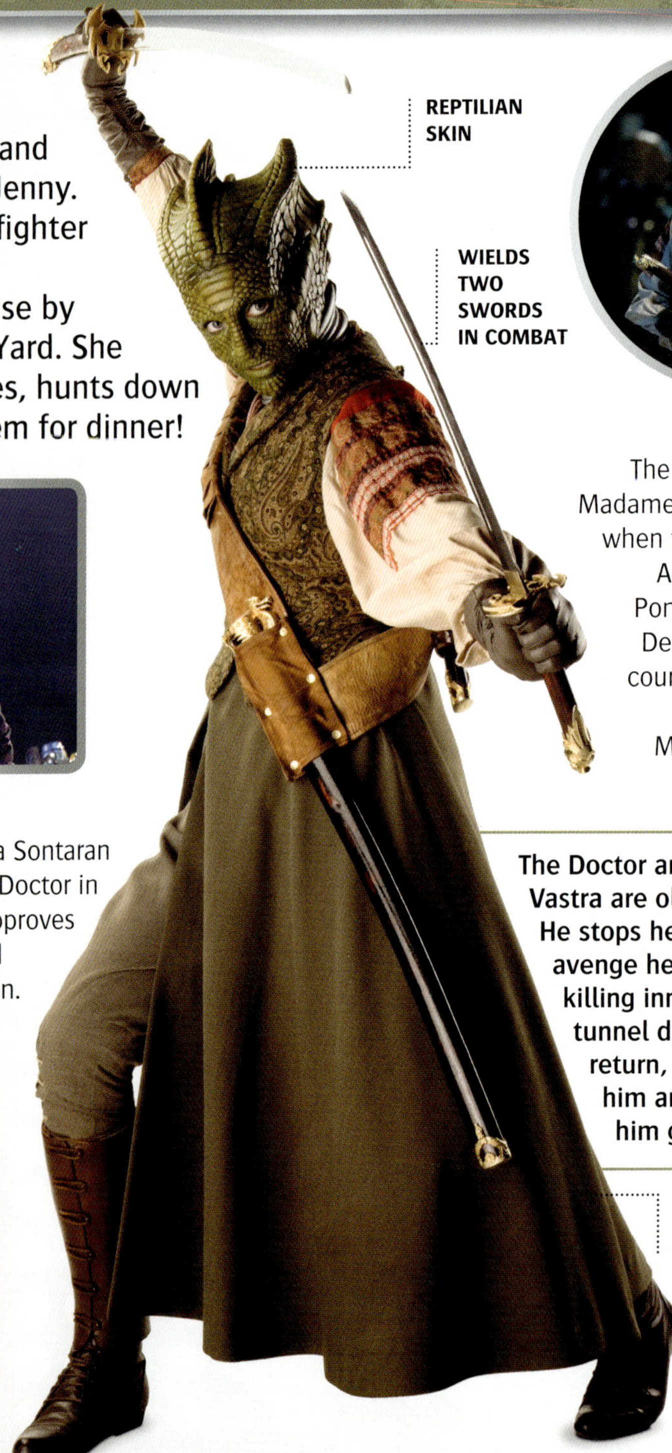

LAST STAND
The Doctor turns to Madame Vastra for help when trying to rescue Amy and Melody Pond from asteroid Demon's Run. She courageously fights the Headless Monks to protect Amy's baby.

DOCTOR DUTY
Madame Vastra, Jenny and a Sontaran called Strax watch over the Doctor in Victorian England. She disapproves of his desire to be alone and thinks he needs a companion.

The Doctor and Madame Vastra are old friends. He stops her trying to avenge her sisters by killing innocent tunnel diggers. In return, she protects him and gives him guidance.

DATA FILE
ORIGIN:
EARTH
SPECIAL ABILITIES:
SWORD-FIGHTING, CRACKING CASES, EATING CRIMINALS
DOCTORS MET:
11TH

MADGE ARWELL
NO ORDINARY HOUSEWIFE!

Kind-hearted Madge Arwell is wife to Reg and mother to Lily and Cyril. Her life takes an unexpected turn when she comes to the aid of a spaceman in a field. Promising to repay her kindness, the spaceman (aka the Doctor) returns years later to give her family a Christmas present like no other!

1940s BOB

1940s COAT WORN OVER NIGHTDRESS IN HASTE

DATA FILE

HOMEWORLD: EARTH

SPECIAL ABILITIES: PICKING LOCKS WITH PINS, TRANSPORTING THE SOULS OF THE TREES IN HER HEAD

DOCTORS MET: 11TH

MISSING IN ACTION
Reg's Lancaster Bomber is lost during World War II. Madge is devastated and can't bring herself to tell her children their dad won't be home for Christmas.

RESCUE MISSION
The Doctor's gift is a portal to another world. When Lily and Cyril vanish through it, Madge follows, determined to rescue them. Her steely resolve saves not only them but also Reg and a whole planet of endangered trees.

In order to protect her children from the London Blitz, Madge takes them to stay in their Uncle Digby's country house – a grand, old building with an eccentric new caretaker called the Doctor!

MARTHA JONES
CAPABLE COMPANION

Martha was a medical student when she first met the Doctor. After saving his life from a blood-sucking Plasmavore, she was invited aboard the TARDIS and soon fell in love with her travelling companion and her new life. Bold and brainy in equal measure, she fought against some of the Doctor's most deadly enemies.

MARTHA'S UNIT CALL SIGN IS "GREYHOUND 6"

ALL-BLACK UNIT UNIFORM

BREAKING AWAY
After helping to save the world from the Master, Martha decided to stop travelling to look after her family. She also needed time to get over her unrequited love for the Doctor.

DATA FILE
ORIGIN:
LONDON, EARTH
OCCUPATION:
DOCTOR, ALIEN HUNTER
DOCTORS MET:
10TH

THE JONESES
When Martha's father Clive, mother Francine and sister Tish are arrested and held at gunpoint by the Master, Martha fears for their lives. She also realises the dangers of being associated with the Doctor.

Martha's adventures continued on Earth when she joined UNIT as a fully qualified doctor. She helped them fight off Dalek and Sontaran invasions, before being persuaded by husband Mickey Smith to become a freelance alien hunter!

THE MASTER
ROGUE TIME LORD

Once childhood friends on Gallifrey, the Master grew up to become the Doctor's archenemy. He turned mad when he looked into the Untempered Schism. Like the Doctor, he stole a TARDIS and left to explore the universe. But unlike the Doctor, the Master wants to conquer worlds and wreak destruction.

DATA FILE

HOMEWORLD:
GALLIFREY

SPECIAL ABILITIES:
REGENERATING, CAUSING HAVOC, BECOMING HUMAN

DOCTORS MET:
3RD, 4TH, 5TH, 6TH, 7TH, 8TH, 10TH

After dying, the Master is resurrected by the Time Lords to fight in the Time War. However, he flees to the end of the universe instead and hides as a human.

OLD RIVALS
As Time Lords, and with the ability to regenerate, the Master and the Doctor have faced each other in many incarnations. The Master is constantly tormented by the sound of drums, as a result of looking into the Time Vortex.

VOTE SAXON
Pretending to be likeable politician Harold Saxon, the Master worms his way into Downing Street. Once in control, he orders deadly Toclafane to kill one tenth of mankind.

MAX CAPRICORN

CEO OF MAX CAPRICORN CRUISELINERS

Max Capricorn is a rich and powerful cyborg who owns a luxury starliner business. When his company fails, he is voted out by his own board. In revenge, he plans to crash one of their spaceships, *Titanic*, into Earth, wiping out mankind so that the board members will be jailed for mass-murder.

HEAVENLY HOST
Max is aided by robots called the Heavenly Host. Originally designed to provide tourist information, they have been reprogrammed by Max to perform only one function – kill any witnesses of his crimes!

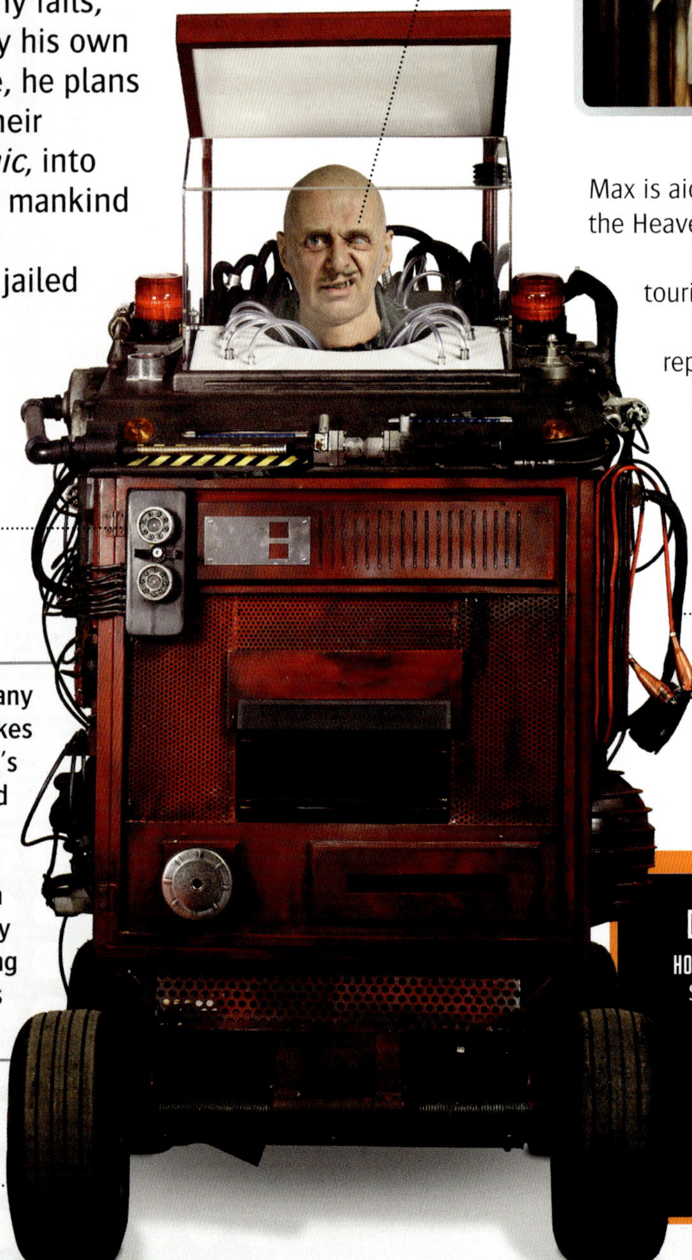

Running a company for 176 years takes its toll on Max's body. He is forced to become a cyborg in a society that hates them and hides away for years, running his business by hologram.

DATA FILE

HOMEWORLD:
STO

SPECIAL ABILITIES:
LONGEVITY, INTRIGUE, POWER

DOCTORS MET:
10TH

MEDDLING MONK
TIME TWISTER

The Monk is from the same homeworld as the Doctor, the planet Gallifrey. He likes to break the golden rule of space and time travel and chooses to interfere with the course of history. To teach him a lesson, the Doctor breaks the dimensional circuit of the Monk's TARDIS.

BAD HABIT
The Monk keeps a diary of his meddling. One entry talks of meeting the Italian painter and sculptor Leonardo da Vinci and discussing powered flight hundreds of years before the aeroplane is invented.

TRAPPED
The First Doctor's companion, Vicki, discovers a Viking's helmet. The Doctor deduces that it is 1066, the year of both the Viking and Norman invasions in Britain and suspects someone is up to no good.

The Monk delights in changing history. He finds it funny and does not care. It is not known what happens to the Monk after the Time War that wiped out Gallifrey and all the Time Lords.

DATA FILE
HOMEWORLD:
GALLIFREY

SPECIAL ABILITIES:
TIME TRAVEL, MEDDLING IN TIME

DOCTORS MET:
1st

MELANIE BUSH
ENERGETIC COMPANION

Better known as Mel, Melanie Bush is a young computer expert who relishes her adventures in the TARDIS. Bright and breezy, Mel is always full of energy and has a tendency to look on the bright side of things. She also has a natural curiosity, a trait which often gets her into danger.

DATA FILE
ORIGIN: PEASE POTTAGE, ENGLAND, EARTH

OCCUPATION: COMPUTER PROGRAMMER

DOCTORS MET: 6TH, 7TH

MULTIPLE MELS
On Lakertya, with the help of the Tetraps, wayward time lady the Rani impersonates Mel in order to gain the trust of the newly-regenerated Doctor. The real Mel has a tough job convincing him she's the real thing!

A fitness fanatic, Mel keeps trying to get the burly Sixth Doctor to eat more healthily and get some exercise. She eventually leaves the TARDIS to travel with loveable rogue, Sabalom Glitz, determined to keep him on the straight and narrow.

MERCY HARTIGAN

CONTROLLER OF THE CYBERKING

UMBRELLA PROTECTS FROM SNOW

Once the matron of a Victorian workhouse, Miss Hartigan forms an alliance with a group of Cybermen. Angry and bitter, she resents men's dominance over women and looks to her "knights in shining armour" to liberate her. However, she is shocked when the Cybermen betray her and turn her into their CyberKing!

FESTIVE VICTORIAN OUTFIT

FULL-LENGTH DRESS

ROBOT REVENGE
Instead of losing her human emotions, Miss Hartigan's strong mind dominates the CyberKing. Angry and defiant, she causes the giant robot to stomp all over London!

To save millions from being converted into Cybermen, the Doctor breaks Miss Hartigan's mental connection with the CyberKing. She is so horrified at what she has become that she ends up destroying both her Cybermen servants and herself.

DATA FILE

ORIGIN:
LONDON, ENGLAND

SPECIAL ABILITIES:
UNUSUALLY STRONG MIND

DOCTORS MET:
10TH

MICKEY SMITH
TALENTED COMPANION

Mickey was the devoted boyfriend of Rose Tyler who all but lost her when she went off travelling with the Doctor. A bit of a no-hoper, Mickey is at first timid and cowardly in the face of alien threats, but shows a great talent for hacking into advanced computer systems.

GOOD WITH COMPUTERS

LOVES FOOTBALL

DATA FILE

ORIGIN:
LONDON, ENGLAND

SPECIAL ABILITIES:
COMPUTER-HACKER, ALIEN HUNTER

DOCTORS MET:
10TH

DELETING CYBERMEN
After fighting the newly created Cybermen on a parallel Earth, Mickey reveals his braver side. He decides to stay behind to help rid the world of the emotionless cyborgs.

CLOCKWORK ALERT
Mickey's first trip in the TARDIS takes him to the *SS Madame de Pompadour* in the far future. Wandering around the spaceship's corridors, both he and Rose are soon attacked by the vessel's clockwork maintenance robots!

A more heroic and grown-up Mickey eventually returns to our universe where he marries another of the Tenth Doctor's companions, Martha Jones. The pair hunt down dangerous aliens on Earth.

THE MINOTAUR
PRISONER IN SPACE

A huge, horned beast, the Minotaur stomps through the corridors of a strange hotel. In reality, the building is an automated prison, built by a race that had once worshipped the creature before turning against it. The prison is programmed to trap other life forms, converting their faith into food for the Minotaur.

After being trapped for thousands of years, the Minotaur wants to die, but is unable to as its instinct to feed is too strong. In the end, the Doctor manages to sever its source of faith energy, allowing the creature to die at last.

NIGHTMARE HOTEL
Desperate not to become another of the Minotaur's victims, the Doctor and his companions hide in the hotel's rooms, each of which contains someone's worst nightmare!

DATA FILE

HOMEWORLD: UNKNOWN

SPECIAL ABILITIES: FEEDS ON FAITH ENERGY

DOCTORS MET: 11TH

MORBIUS
TIME LORD WAR CRIMINAL

A Time Lord from the planet Gallifrey, Morbius was a ruthless dictator. Originally he once led the High Council of the Time Lords, and he wanted to use their powers to conquer planets rather than just observe them. He had millions of followers and admirers.

THE CULT OF MORBIUS

The Doctor recognises a model of Morbius' head when the TARDIS arrives on the planet Karn. Morbius and his followers – known as the Cult of Morbius – had come to Karn to steal the Elixir of Life so that they could be immortal.

For a long time it was thought that Morbius was dead, killed for his crimes. His brain, however, survived, thanks to a neurosurgeon called Mehendri Solon.

SURGEON SOLON

Solon is a brilliant Earth neurosurgeon who hides away on the planet Karn. He is responsible for piecing together a new body to host the brain of Morbius.

DATA FILE

HOMEWORLD: GALLIFREY, ORIGINALLY

SPECIAL ABILITIES: REGENERATION

DOCTORS MET: 4TH

MOVELLANS

BEAUTIFUL ANDROIDS

The Movellans are a race of androids that generally hide the fact that they are not human. Physically striking, they are all incredibly strong and can lift great weights without any effort at all. For many years, the Movellans were locked in a war with the Daleks.

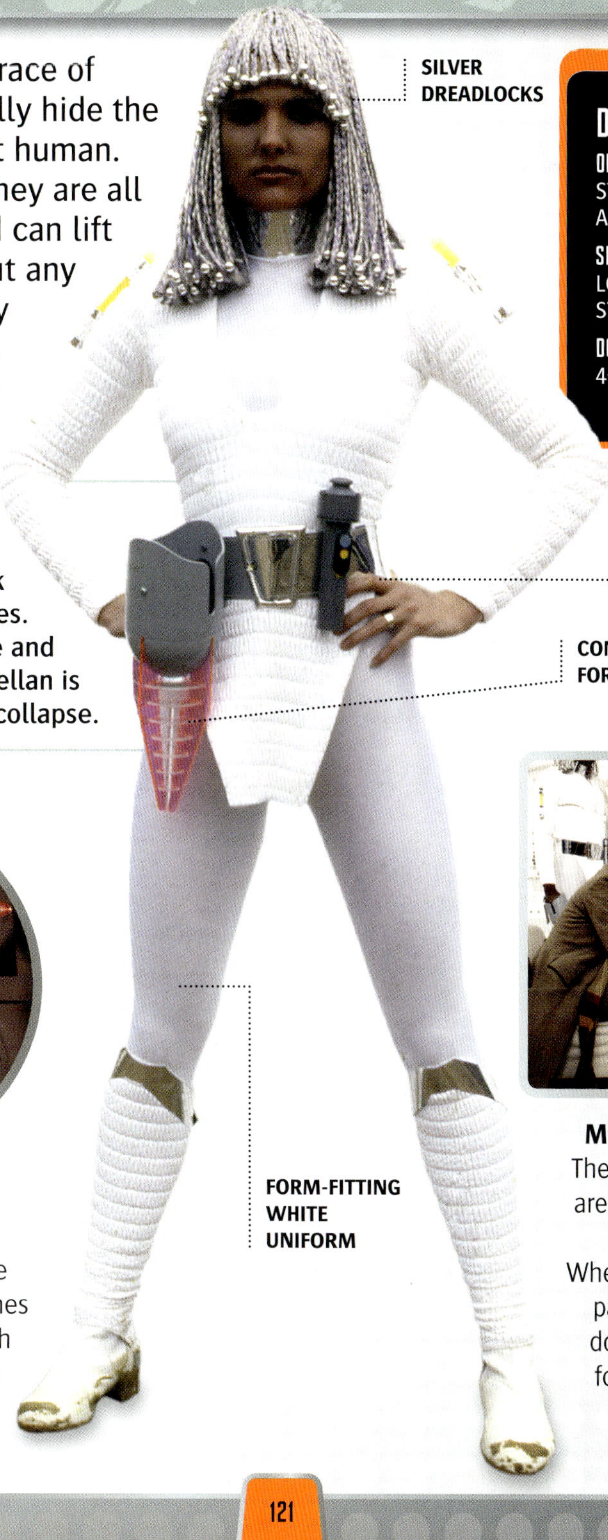

DATA FILE

ORIGIN:
STAR SYSTEM 4X ALPHA 4

SPECIAL ABILITIES:
LOGICAL, PHYSICAL STRENGTH

DOCTORS MET:
4TH

A design fault of these androids is the visible power pack attached to their bodies. It is easy to remove and without it, the Movellan is powerless and will collapse.

DUEL WITH DALEKS

The logical machine minds of the Movellans are their downfall when it comes to fighting the Daleks. Both races are, however, unable to beat the other due to their logical tactics.

MOVELLAN SPACESHIP

The Movellans spaceships are striking, as the Doctor and Romana discover. When landing on a planet, part of the ship will drill down into the earth as a form of camouflage and also defence.

THE MOXX OF BALHOON

OBSERVER OF EARTHDEATH

A representative of the solicitors Jolco and Jolco, the Moxx of Balhoon is one of the many distinguished guests aboard Platform One who have come to witness the natural destruction of planet Earth. A shrivelled, goblin-like creature, the Moxx is unable to walk and floats around on a special anti-gravity chair.

SPITTING SURPRISE

As a formal greeting, the Moxx of Balhoon gives the gift of bodily saliva. Unfortunately for Rose, she is the one who ends up with spit in her eye.

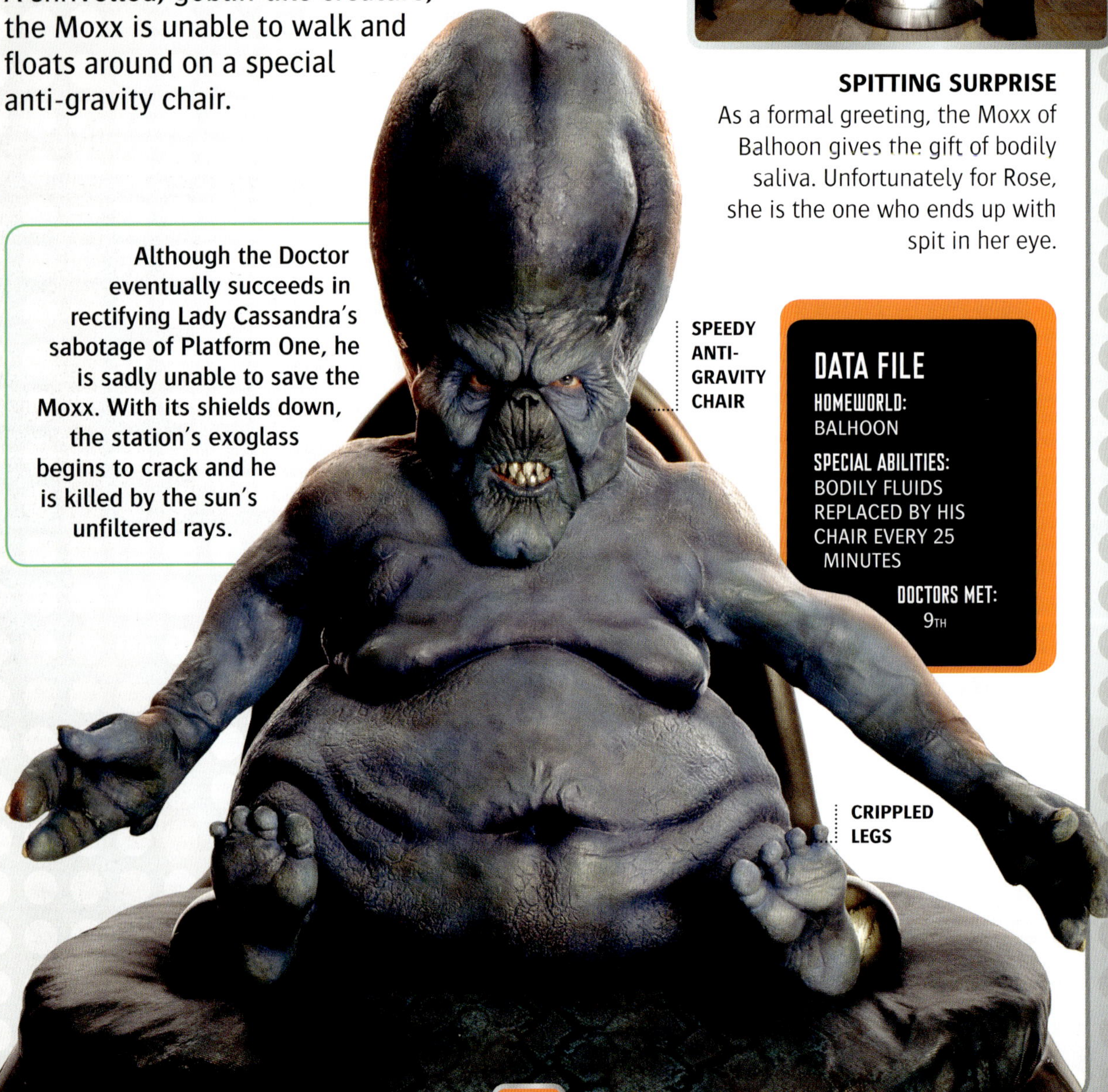

Although the Doctor eventually succeeds in rectifying Lady Cassandra's sabotage of Platform One, he is sadly unable to save the Moxx. With its shields down, the station's exoglass begins to crack and he is killed by the sun's unfiltered rays.

DATA FILE

HOMEWORLD: BALHOON

SPECIAL ABILITIES: BODILY FLUIDS REPLACED BY HIS CHAIR EVERY 25 MINUTES

DOCTORS MET: 9TH

MUTTS

MUTANT INSECTOID SOLONIANS

The humanoid Solonians on the planet Solos are undergoing a long evolutionary process, unknown to themselves. One stage in the terrifying transformation produces insect-like mutant creatures, who become known as "Mutts", by those who look down on and don't understand them.

SOLONIAN STRUGGLES

When the Doctor arrives on Solos, the planet is in turmoil. Many humans in the Solos-based Earth colony, and some Solonians, despise the Mutts, believing them to be diseased, and want them wiped out.

A new evolutionary stage in the life of an Insectoid Solonian occurs every five hundred years, as the seasons on Solos alter. In the summer, the "Mutt" will eventually change into a beautiful and powerful super-being.

DATA FILE

HOMEWORLD: SOLOS

SPECIAL ABILITIES: METAMORPHOSES

DOCTORS MET: 3RD

NIMON

PARASITIC BULL CREATURES

The imposing Nimon treat whole populations of planets as their food supply. Typically, a Nimon will arrive on a planet, set itself up as a god to be worshipped and then start demanding sacrifices. On Skonnos, the planet's leader Soldeed serves the Nimon. He believes that the creature will give him power and riches in return for his help.

HORNS THAT EMIT AN ENERGY BEAM

BULL FACE

The Nimon are a technically advanced race. They are able to create black holes linked to any planet they choose, and travel between worlds in transmat capsules.

RESEMBLES MINOTAUR FROM GREEK LEGENDS ON EARTH

DATA FILE

HOMEWORLD:
SEVERAL, INCLUDING SKONNOS AND CRINOTH

SPECIAL ABILITIES:
CONVERTING HUMANS INTO ENERGY, INTERGALACTIC TRAVEL

DOCTORS MET:
4TH

SACRIFICES

The Nimon claim humans as sacrifices and drain their life force for energy to sustain them. Once depleted, all that is left of the human is an empty husk.

NYSSA
TRAKENITE COMPANION

The Fourth Doctor meets Nyssa on Traken, a peaceful world that had been invaded by the dying Master who was desperate to prolong his life. The gentle daughter of an eminent scientist called Tremas, Nyssa inherits her father's intellect and helps the Doctor rid her world of the renegade Time Lord.

After travelling with both the Fourth and Fifth Doctors, it is Nyssa's caring nature that influences her decision to leave him. She chooses to stay on Terminus and use her scientific skills to develop a cure for the fatal Lazar's disease.

MEETING THE MASTER
When her father disappears, Nyssa goes in search of him. She is horrified to discover that not only had the Master taken over his body, but he had also destroyed her entire world, meaning Nyssa is the last of the Trakenites.

DATA FILE
HOMEWORLD: TRAKEN

OCCUPATION: BIOELECTRONICS EXPERT

DOCTORS MET: 4TH, 5TH

OGRI
BLOODTHIRSTY STONES

The Ogri are large silicon-based life forms from the repulsive swamp planet Ogros. Resembling large standing stones, they can live for centuries, living off amino acids. While on Earth, the Ogri need blood globulin to survive. An Ogri can absorb the blood of a human in seconds.

Three Ogri arrive on Earth with a criminal called Cessair of Diplos. They end up forming part of a stone circle called the Nine Travellers, confusing people because their number changed between surveys.

CESSAIR OF DIPLOS

Wanted for murder and theft, Cessair of Diplos comes to Earth to avoid capture. She assumes a number of identities across centuries, while the Ogri serve and carry out her commands.

DATA FILE

HOMEWORLD:
OGROS IN THE TAU CETI SYSTEM

SPECIAL ABILITIES:
DRAINING LIFE FORMS OF BLOOD

DOCTORS MET:
4TH

OGRONS
UNINTELLIGENT SERVANT RACE

The Ogrons are lumbering ape creatures with little intelligence, making them loyal servants to their masters. Living in scattered communities on one of the outer planets, they act as a simple and effective police force. They are honest and have very simple needs.

In the 22nd century, the Daleks use the Ogrons to keep humans under control. Centuries later, the Master works with them to start a war between humans and Draconians – reptilian humanoids from Draconia.

DATA FILE
HOMEWORLD:
THE OUTER PLANETS
SPECIAL ABILITIES:
STRENGTH, STAMINA
DOCTORS MET:
3RD

DICTATOR DALEKS
Daleks probably use the stupidity of the Ogron race to their advantage. An Ogron will never reveal any Dalek plans and will carry out orders without question.

SO LONG, OGRON
The Third Doctor escapes the clutches of the Ogrons at Auderly House, where a world peace conference was due to be held.

OMEGA
BETRAYED TIME LORD

Omega is the Time Lord regarded as a hero for giving the people of Gallifrey the ability to travel through time. It was widely believed that the stellar engineer died when he blew up a star in order to harness its power for time travel, but in fact he lives on, trapped inside a lonely anti-matter universe. Alone and abandoned, he seeks revenge.

DATA FILE

HOMEWORLD: GALLIFREY, ORIGINALLY

SPECIAL ABILITIES: STELLAR ENGINEERING

DOCTORS MET: 3RD, 5TH

GELL GUARDS
In his anti-matter world, Omega commands Gell Guards – horrific anti-matter creatures of his own creation. The beings invade UNIT HQ and take the building and the Doctor back to Omega's world.

ELABORATE HEADPIECE

ANTI-MATTER BODY

Driven insane from his exile in his anti-matter world, Omega plans to return to the proper universe. But as anti-matter himself, he is unable to exist in a positive-matter universe.

BODY COPY
In another attempt to return to the positive-matter world, Omega steals the Doctor's biodata from the Matrix on Gallifrey. His return is short-lived as Omega is destroyed on Earth.

THE OOD
HIVE-MINDED HUMANOIDS

A race of gentle, tentacle-faced telepaths, the Ood lived in peaceful harmony until the arrival of the Halpen Family. These entrepreneurial tycoons enslaved the Ood and sold them throughout the Human Empire. They were set free by the Doctor in 4126 AD.

Each Ood is born with an external hindbrain containing the creature's memories and personality. Unlike the forebrains in their heads, the Ood carry their delicate hindbrains in their hands.

THE NEPHEW
An Ood known as Nephew was transported to a living asteroid called House and came under the entity's psychic control. Nephew has the scary ability to drain people's minds from their bodies!

RED EYE
On Krop Tor, the Ood's telepathic field comes under the psychic possession of the Beast. Somehow, as a sign of their possession, their eyes glow red and they act in ways that, for a peaceful race, are unnaturally violent.

DATA FILE
HOMEWORLD: OOD SPHERE
SPECIAL ABILITIES: TELEPATHY, POWER OF PROPHECY
DOCTORS MET: 10TH, 11TH

PATCHWORK PEOPLE
TIME LORD TRAPPERS

Auntie and Uncle are Patchwork People. Their bodies are Frankenstein-like collections of Time Lord body parts that have been crudely stitched together. They live in a TARDIS junkyard on a talking asteroid called House and act as his servants.

HUNGRY HOUSE

The Patchwork People see House as their saviour. He mends and nourishes them and in turn they do his will, luring Time Lords to their doom so House can eat their TARDISes.

Auntie and Uncle were once travellers who came through the Rift. But they have been patched up so many times that nothing recognisable remains of their original selves.

DATA FILE

HOMEWORLD: HOUSE

SPECIAL ABILITIES: TRICKING TIME LORDS

DOCTORS MET: 11TH

PEG DOLLS

LIVING TOYS

The Peg Dolls were brought to life by the psycho-kinetic powers of a young boy called George. Really an alien Tenza, George has the ability to send everything he's afraid of into a doll's house in his cupboard. The dolls hunt down people and transform them into dolls.

DATA FILE

ORIGIN:
EARTH

SPECIAL ABILITIES:
TRANSFORMING OTHER BEINGS INTO DOLLS

DOCTORS MET:
11TH

The transformation into a Peg Doll is quick. First, the victim's hands get bigger and turn to wood, followed by the rest of the body. When Amy and Rory find themselves in the doll's house, Amy is caught and becomes a doll – ending up in a state of living death.

NO MORE NIGHT TERRORS

After George himself appears in the doll's house, the toys surround him and threaten to transform him. When his Dad reassures him that he is loved, though, his fears disappear and everyone is returned to normal.

PERI BROWN
AMERICAN STUDENT COMPANION

While on holiday in Lanzarote, American botany student Perpugilliam "Peri" Brown is saved from drowning by the Doctor's companion, Turlough. Adventurous Peri gleefully accepts the Doctor's invitation to travel with him and Turlough.

SIXTH DOCTOR
Peri finds it tough going when the Doctor regenerates into his explosive and unstable sixth incarnation. Luckily, the Doctor eventually settles down and the pair become good friends.

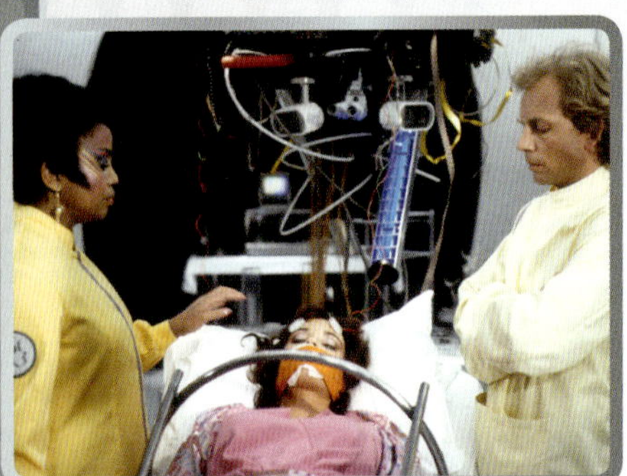

BRAIN TRANSFER
Put on trial by the Time Lords, the Doctor is shown evidence that his meddling has led to Peri's death. The brain of Mentor Kiv has seemingly been transplanted into her body!

After their many adventures fighting the likes of Cybermen, Gastropods and Sontarans, the Doctor is distraught at his companion's death. Happily, he later discovers that the evidence had been faked – Peri had in fact married the boisterous warrior King Yrcanos!

DATA FILE
ORIGIN:
USA, EARTH
OCCUPATION:
STUDENT
DOCTORS MET:
2nd, 5th, 6th

PETE TYLER
ROSE TYLER'S FATHER

Rose's Dad Pete dies in a car crash when she is just six months old. She grows up hearing stories from her mum Jackie about how clever and brilliant he was. But in truth he is a hopeless dreamer whose daft money-making schemes never work.

REUNITED
Pete meets his grown-up daughter when she goes back in time and saves his life. But it causes a wound in time that can only be healed by his death.

PETE'S WORLD
In a parallel universe, Pete is a successful and wealthy businessman. He works undercover to stop Cybus Industries creating Cybermen and saves Rose from being sucked into the Void.

PARALLEL WORLD VERSION OF PETE TYLER

Jackie is always telling Pete he's useless. He wishes he could be a proper businessman and a better husband and father. However, when Jackie meets the parallel world version of Pete, the two are given a second chance together. They fall in love again and go on to have a son – Tony.

DATA FILE

HOMEWORLD:
EARTH, PARALLEL EARTH

SPECIAL ABILITIES:
SELF-SACRIFICE, FIGHTING CYBERMEN

DOCTORS MET:
9TH, 10TH

PIG SLAVES

HOG-FACED HENCHMEN

Pig Slaves are the savage servants of the Daleks. They are the horrific result of a genetic experiment in which the Daleks merged humans with pigs in the sewers of New York City. Their job is to kidnap other humans for the Daleks to experiment on as part of their quest for evolution and survival.

DATA FILE

ORIGIN:
EARTH

SPECIAL ABILITIES:
KIDNAPPING, KILLING, FOLLOWING DALEK ORDERS

DOCTORS MET:
10TH

Daleks select the least intelligent humans to become Pig Slaves, saving clever people to become Dalek-Human soldiers. Once converted, they forget their humanity and act like wild beasts.

LUCKY LASZLO

Laszlo is working at a theatre in New York when he is ambushed by Pig Slaves. They take him to the Daleks to be converted into a Pig Slave, but Laszlo escapes before they take his mind and he can still talk.

THE CULT OF SKARO

The Pig Slaves' masters are an elite group of Daleks known as the Cult of Skaro. Pig Slaves obey these Daleks without question, dragging people down into the New York sewers to be transformed.

PLASMAVORES
BLOOD-SUCKING SHAPE-SHIFTERS

The Plasmavores are a vicious race of shape-changing aliens who survive by draining the blood of other life forms, leaving them for dead. By assimilating their blood, they have the ability to mimic the internal structure of their victims' bodies – a talent which enables the creatures to avoid detection.

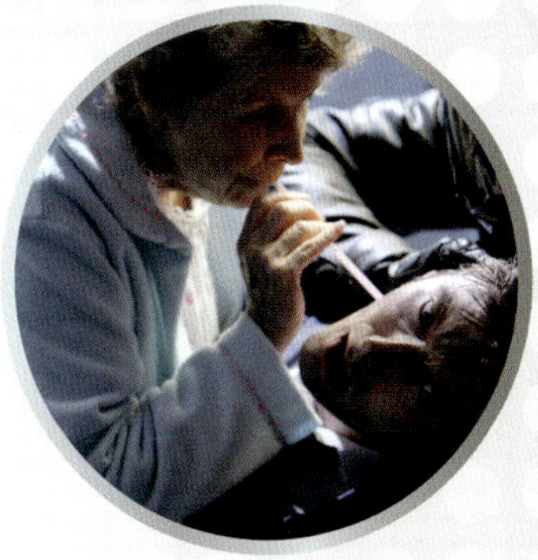

DRAINING THE DOCTOR
With the Judoon on her trail, Florence drinks the Doctor's blood, believing it will make her appear human, thus hiding her real identity. She gets a shock when the Judoon's scanners say otherwise!

JUDOON ARMY
The Judoon invade Royal Hope Hospital on Earth in their search for a rogue criminal Plasmavore operating under the alias of Florence Finnegan. She is accused of murdering the Child Princess of Padrivole Regency Nine.

Florence is assisted by two Slabs – solid leather drones who hold down her victims while she feasts on their blood. However, she cannot run from the Judoon for long, and is eventually executed by them for her crimes.

X INDICATES FLORENCE HAS SUPPOSEDLY BEEN APPROVED AS BEING HUMAN BY THE JUDOON

DATA FILE

ORIGIN:
UNKNOWN

SPECIAL ABILITIES:
MIMICKING OTHER LIFE FORMS

DOCTORS MET:
10TH

POLLY WRIGHT
CONFIDENT COMPANION

A bright, fun-loving girl from 1960s London, Polly is the secretary to Professor Brett, the creator of WOTAN. When the supercomputer decides to take over humanity, Polly is one of many who is hypnotised into constructing its war machines. Luckily she survives the ordeal, and stays with the First Doctor after helping him defeat WOTAN.

DATA FILE

ORIGIN:
ENGLAND

OCCUPATION:
PERSONAL ASSISTANT

DOCTORS MET:
1st, 2nd

MOONWALK
When the TARDIS lands on the moon, Polly is excited about taking a walk across the lunar surface. It's not long though before she comes up against the invading Cybermen.

TALL TALES
Polly first sneaks aboard the TARDIS with Ben Jackson in order to test the Doctor's tales about his adventures in space and time. They soon become embroiled with a smuggling ring in Cornwall in the 17th century!

Polly copes with many strange experiences during her travels. After witnessing the First Doctor's regeneration, she encounters the malevolent Macra and is nearly turned into a fish person. In the end, she leaves the Doctor to return to a normal life in London.

PRISONER ZERO

SHAPE-SHIFTING ALIEN CRIMINAL

A prisoner of the Atraxi, Prisoner Zero is a gelatinous serpent creature that escapes to Earth through a crack in time, hiding out in the house of Amy Pond. As a shape-shifting multi-form, it can copy the identities of more than one creature at the same time, thus avoiding capture.

ONE MAN AND HIS DOG
When the Doctor draws Amy's attention to a room concealed by a perception filter, Prisoner Zero shows itself, disguised as an angry man with an equally ferocious-looking dog.

Before it can copy another life form, Prisoner Zero needs to link with it psychically. This proves simple to achieve with the unconscious patients in a nearby coma ward. Prisoner Zero can even assume the form of a creature that is being dreamt about.

DATA FILE

ORIGIN:
UNKNOWN

SPECIAL ABILITIES:
ASSUMING THE APPEARANCE OF OTHER BEINGS, CREATING PERCEPTION FILTERS

DOCTORS MET:
11TH

PROFESSOR EDWARD TRAVERS
BRITISH EXPLORER

Professor Edward Travers is an explorer. He is searching for the Yeti in the Himalayas when he becomes caught up with the robot Yeti attacks and the Great Intelligence. Forty years later he reactivates a Yeti and ends up fighting the Great Intelligence again in London's Underground, alongside his daughter Anne – who is a scientific advisor for the British army.

THERMAL HAT

THICK LAYERS FOR HUNTING IN COLD CLIMES

HUNTING RIFLE

Travers has always believed that the Abominable Snowman exists. Quick to judge, when his friend is killed on an expedition, he initially thinks it is the Doctor who did it.

YETI ATTACK
Forty years after his first encounter with the Yeti and the Doctor, Travers sells one of the unanimated Yeti to a museum. When he reactivates one of the control spheres, he brings back the threat of the Yeti to Earth.

DATA FILE

ORIGIN:
EARTH

SPECIAL ABILITIES:
EXPLORING

DOCTORS MET:
2ND

PROFESSOR LAZARUS

CREATOR OF THE GMD

An elderly scientist, Professor Richard Lazarus uses his great invention, the Genetic Manipulation Device (GMD), to make himself thirty years younger. During the process, however, he unwittingly brings to the surface a series of molecules in his DNA which had stayed dormant throughout humanity's evolution. As a result, Lazarus is transformed into a savage, multi-limbed monster.

DATA FILE

ORIGIN:
EARTH

SPECIAL ABILITIES:
MUTATING BETWEEN HUMAN AND ARTHROPODAL FORMS, DRAINING PEOPLE'S LIFE FORCE

DOCTORS MET:
10TH

DINNER TIME
With its DNA fluctuating wildly, the Lazarus creature needs huge amounts of energy to maintain its mutated form. To satisfy its appetite, it sucks the life force from its victims, leaving behind a shrunken husk.

30 YEARS YOUNGER
Professor Lazarus may have made himself younger, but the process produces disastrous consequences.

In monster form, Lazarus chases Martha and Tish inside Southwark Cathedral. The Doctor uses his sonic screwdriver to magnify the resonance of a pipe organ, causing the creature to plummet to its death.

PYROVILES

FIRE-BREATHING ROCK MONSTERS

Huge creatures composed of rock and lava, the Pyroviles landed on Earth thousands of years ago, shattering on impact. On reawakening, they start reconstituting themselves by causing humans to breathe in their dust, transforming them into living stone. They plan to convert millions more, by using the power of the volcano Vesuvius.

SHOOTS FLAMES FROM MOUTH

FORM MADE OF ROCK AND LAVA

VERY HOT

CAN BE OVER 10 METRES (33 FEET) TALL

The Doctor faces a terrible dilemma. He can either allow the Pyroviles to take over the human race or destroy the creatures by triggering an eruption. In the end, he causes Vesuvius to erupt and the city of Pompeii is destroyed.

DATA FILE

HOMEWORLD:
PYROVILLIA

SPECIAL ABILITIES:
TURNING OTHER BEINGS INTO PYROVILES, BREATHING FIRE AND TURNING PEOPLE TO ASH

DOCTORS MET:
10TH

STONE SISTERS
In Pompeii, the Doctor encounters the High Priestess of the Sibylline Sisterhood. He discovers she is halfway to becoming a Pyrovile and has almost completely turned to stone.

RACNOSS
SEMI-HUMANOID SPIDER CREATURES

Born starving, the Racnoss are ten-limbed omnivores from the Dark Times who were believed to have been wiped out during a war with the Fledgling Empires. The last of their kind, the Racnoss Empress, returns to Earth billions of years later, eager to free her children – who have been asleep at the centre of the planet all this time.

REVENGE OF THE RACNOSS
While the Racnoss wakes her starving young, her Webstar spaceship descends through Earth's atmosphere. It obeys her order to open fire on the humans below and reduce them to mere meat!

During his battle with the Racnoss, the Doctor travels billions of years back in time and makes a startling discovery. The gravitational force of an escaping Racnoss ship drew rocks towards it as it fled – meaning the creatures were responsible for the creation of Earth!

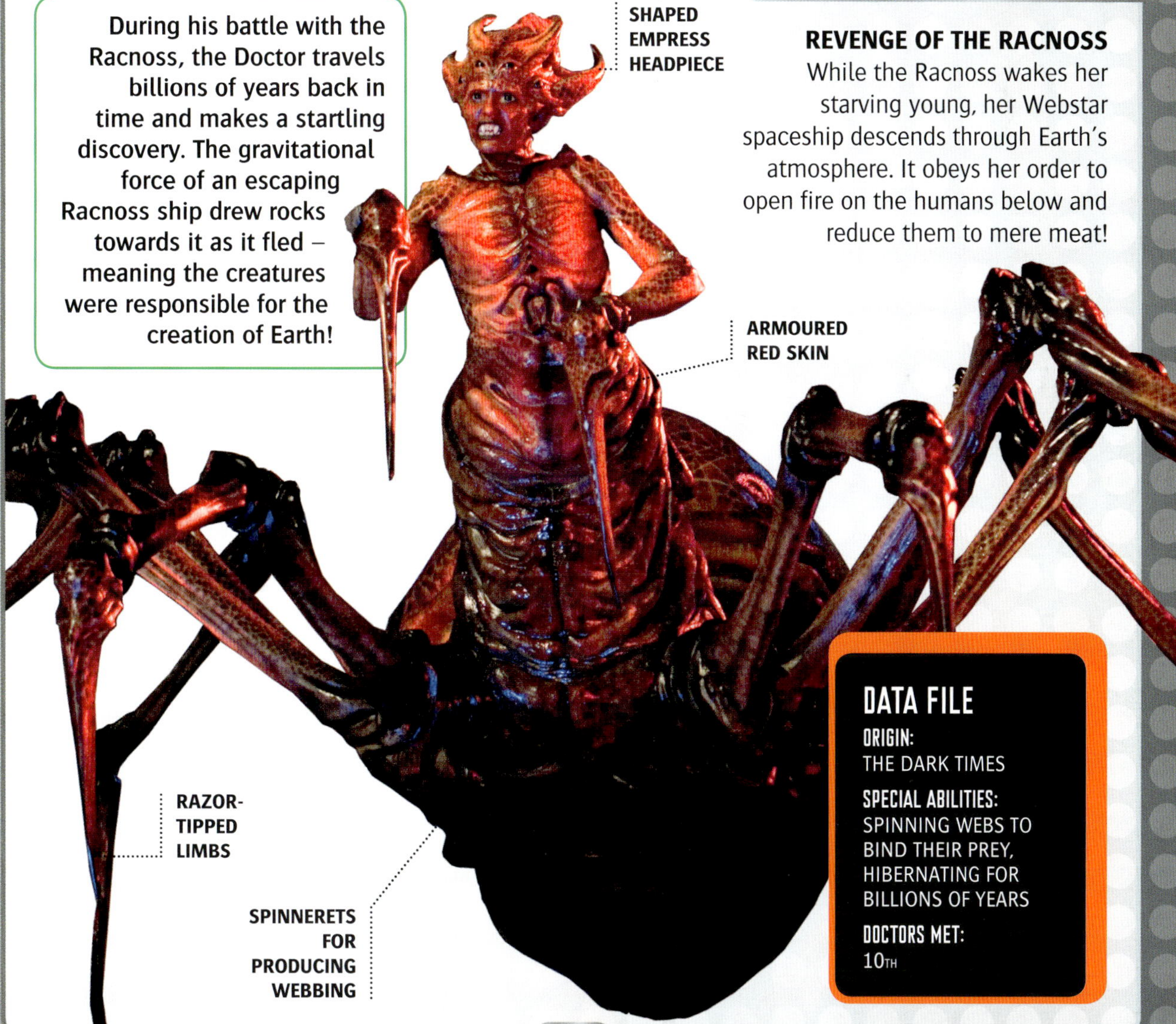

DATA FILE

ORIGIN:
THE DARK TIMES

SPECIAL ABILITIES:
SPINNING WEBS TO BIND THEIR PREY, HIBERNATING FOR BILLIONS OF YEARS

DOCTORS MET:
10TH

THE RANI
DANGEROUS TIME LADY

The Rani is a scientific genius. A Time Lady from Gallifrey, she is exiled when one of her experiments – an enlarged mouse – bites the President and also eats his cat. She has a TARDIS, but what happens to her after the Time War is unknown.

TETRAPS
The Rani uses Tetraps as servants when she is on their home planet of Lakertya. These hairy, bat-like creatures eventually capture their mistress and take her back to their home planet.

COPY CAT
This Time Lady has a sense of humour. To baffle the newly regenerated Seventh Doctor, the Rani dresses up as his companion Mel. For a short time, this confuses the Time Lord.

EVIL SMILE

EYE-CATCHING JACKET

COMMUNICATION AND STORAGE DEVICE

The Rani cares about one thing only – herself. Stylish and incredibly beautiful, she rules the planets Miasimia Goria and Lakertya, using the natives in her experiments.

DATA FILE
HOMEWORLD:
GALLIFREY

SPECIAL ABILITIES:
REGENERATION, CHEMISTRY, DISGUISE

DOCTORS MET:
6TH, 7TH

RASSILON
FOUNDER OF TIME LORD SOCIETY

One of the greatest figures in Time Lord history, Rassilon was originally an engineer and architect who brought the nucleus of a black hole to Gallifrey. Known as the Eye of Harmony, it became as legendary as Rassilon, providing the Time Lords with the eternal energy source they needed for their time-travel.

THE ULTIMATE SANCTION

Rassilon intends to end the Time War by initiating the "Ultimate Sanction" and bringing about the End of Time. Only the Time Lords will survive, becoming creatures of consciousness alone. Luckily, the Doctor succeeds in stopping him.

Brought back to life by the Time Lords, Rassilon is their leader during the Time War. He even finds a way to avoid Gallifrey's seemingly inevitable destruction, eventually confronting the Doctor on Earth.

DATA FILE

HOMEWORLD: GALLIFREY

SPECIAL ABILITIES: GAUNTLET WITH UNUSUAL POWERS

DOCTORS MET: 1st, 2nd, 3rd, 5th, 10th

RASTON WARRIOR ROBOTS
PERFECT KILLING MACHINES

Raston Warrior Robots are the most perfect killing machines ever created. Reacting to the slightest movement, the silver androids can move short distances in the blink of an eye in order to attack their prey. Conveniently, weapons such as sharp arrows and discs are built into their arms. A quick movement will then shoot the chosen armament directly from their hand.

DATA FILE

HOMEWORLD:
UNKNOWN

SPECIAL ABILITIES:
INCREDIBLE SPEED, KILLING CYBERMEN, CAN REFORM WHEN BLOWN UP OR DECAPITATED

DOCTORS MET:
3RD

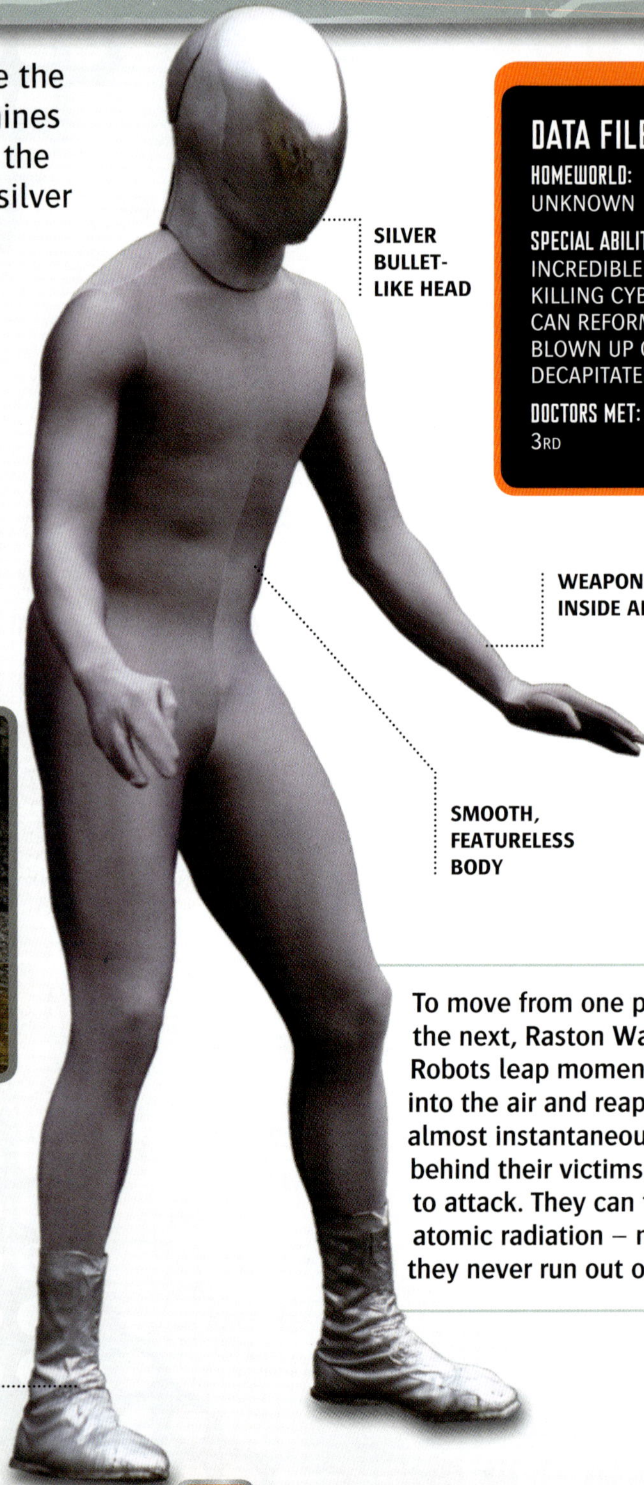

CYBERMEN MASSACRE
While trapped in the Death Zone on Gallifrey, one lone Raston Warrior Robot destroys a whole troop of Cybermen all by itself.

To move from one place to the next, Raston Warrior Robots leap momentarily into the air and reappear almost instantaneously behind their victims, ready to attack. They can feed on atomic radiation – meaning they never run out of energy.

REAPERS
TIME PREDATORS

Terrifying dragon-like creatures, the Reapers search out time paradoxes and "sterilise" the rips in the fabric of time by devouring everyone in sight. The Doctor comes face to face with the predators after Rose Tyler changes history by preventing her dad, Pete, dying in a car accident.

DATA FILE
ORIGIN:
THE TIME VORTEX
SPECIAL ABILITIES:
STERILISING WOUNDS IN TIME
DOCTORS MET:
9TH

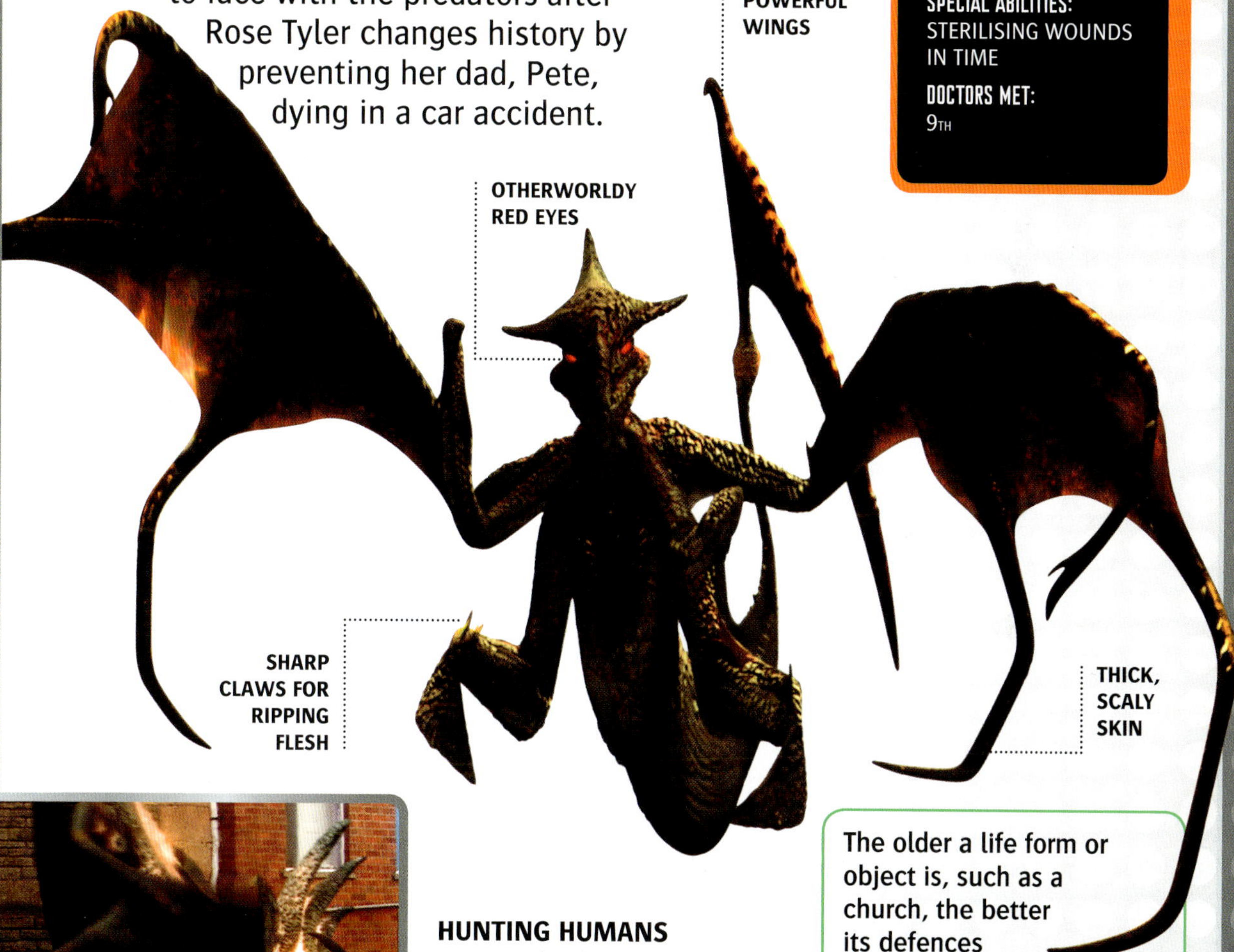

HUNTING HUMANS
As a result of Rose's actions, the Reapers swoop down on wedding guests outside a church with ear-splitting shrieks. The only way to defeat the Reapers is for Pete to sacrifice himself and put time back on the correct path.

The older a life form or object is, such as a church, the better its defences against the Reapers, albeit for a limited amount of time. Temporal paradoxes, such as Rose meeting herself as a baby, only help to make them even stronger.

RIVER SONG
THE DOCTOR'S WIFE

Enigmatic and flirtatious, River Song is a time-travelling archaeology professor constantly meeting the Doctor in the wrong order. He eventually learns that she is Rory and Amy's daughter – the "child of the TARDIS" – so can regenerate, amongst other Time Lord skills. She is also conditioned to be responsible for the Doctor's death, due to her upbringing at the hands of his enemies Madame Kovarian and The Silence.

When River first learns what kind of man the Doctor is, she gives up her remaining regenerations to save him. Although she is imprisoned for later seemingly killing him, she is eventually pardoned and continues on her own adventures, sometimes alongside her Time Lord husband.

DATA FILE

ORIGIN:
DEMON'S RUN ASTEROID

OCCUPATION:
ARCHAEOLOGIST

DOCTORS MET:
10TH, 11TH

RIVER GETS MARRIED
Having overcome her conditioning, River refuses to kill the Doctor and causes time itself to split apart. She ends up marrying him in a resultant alternative timeline, and helps him to cheat death.

SPOILERS!
To keep track of her muddled-up adventures with the Doctor, River Song keeps a special time-traveller's diary. She is careful not to let him read about events in his own future though – in case he comes across spoilers!

ROBOFORMS

ROBOTIC SCAVENGERS

Roboforms are silent scavengers who travel through space alongside more powerful life forms. On Christmas Day 2006, the Roboforms are attracted by the Doctor's regeneration and try to abduct him, intending to use him as a power source. A year later, they are used by the Racnoss Empress to track down and kidnap Donna Noble.

SINISTER SANTAS
Posing as a band of Santas, the Roboforms make an attempt to eliminate the Doctor's defences. They open fire on Rose and Mickey using weapons disguised as musical instruments.

BLACK CLOAK HIDES ALL BUT THEIR FACES

In 102 AD, several undisguised Roboforms join the Pandorica Alliance – a group that wants to trap the Doctor in the Pandorica underground prison, believing that they will stop him from destroying the universe.

ROSE & MICKEY
The Roboforms send a robotic Christmas tree to Rose and Mickey. It can only be stopped using a sonic screwdriver.

DATA FILE

HOMEWORLD:
UNKNOWN

SPECIAL ABILITIES:
TELEPORTATION

DOCTORS MET:
10th, 11th

ROMANA
TIME LORD COMPANION

Romanadvoratrelundar is a Time Lord sent by the White Guardian to help the Doctor assemble the Key to Time, a mythical artefact used to control the universal order. Haughty and conventional, she's initially critical of the Doctor's unusual methods and lack of academic achievement, causing much friction between the two travellers.

After locating the Key, Romana forms a close bond with the Doctor, respecting his knowledge and experience. Ultimately, she realises she has to be her own person and she leaves him to help free the enslaved Tharil race in E-Space.

FLOWING WHITE GOWN

GLAMOROUS FUR STOLE

DATA FILE

HOMEWORLD:
GALLIFREY

SPECIAL ABILITIES:
CAN CHOOSE WHICH FORM SHE REGENERATES INTO

DOCTORS MET:
4TH

ROMANA MK 2
Deciding to regenerate, Romana cheekily models herself on Princess Astra of Atrios, much to the Doctor's annoyance. Luckily, he ends up getting on better with this more playful version of Romana.

RORY WILLIAMS
CARING COMPANION

Amy Pond's long-suffering childhood sweetheart Rory ends up travelling with her aboard the TARDIS. At first rather timid and suspicious of the Doctor, Rory's confidence soon grows and he becomes a more willing adventurer – even though he is apparently killed and brought back to life many times!

Caring and sensitive, Rory remains devoted to Amy and eventually marries her. Together they take on everything from Pirates and Peg Dolls to Silurians and Silents.

CASUAL, SCRUFFY JEANS

CYBERMAN STAND-OFF
When Amy is kidnapped by Madame Kovarian, Rory stops at nothing to get her back. Armed only with the Doctor's sonic screwdriver, he confronts a group of Cybermen and demands to know his wife's whereabouts!

STUCK IN TIME
Rory's travels with the Doctor come to a tragic end when he is zapped back in time by a Weeping Angel. Amy follows him, despite knowing that they will never be able to see the Doctor again.

DATA FILE

ORIGIN:
LEADWORTH, ENGLAND

OCCUPATION:
NURSE

DOCTORS MET:
11TH

ROSE TYLER
COMPASSIONATE COMPANION

Rose was an ordinary shop girl who met the Ninth Doctor after she was attacked by a horde of murderous shop dummies. After helping the Doctor defeat the Nestene Consciousness and its Auton servants, she couldn't resist joining him on his travels. Over time, she grows very close to the battle-scarred Time Lord.

CARING AND KIND-HEARTED

STREETWISE LONDON ORIGINS

ROSE BECOMES TOUGHER AFTER HER TRAVELS WITH THE DOCTOR

DEATH TO THE DALEKS
With the power of the Time Vortex running through her head, Rose once atomised an entire Dalek fleet and its Emperor. She also uses her temporary powers to make Captain Jack immortal!

After an epic battle against the Daleks and Cybermen, Rose becomes trapped in a parallel universe. Determined as ever, she finds a way to return and ends up living her life with a part-human version of the Tenth Doctor.

A HUMAN TOUCH
Rose's compassionate nature is displayed when she is drawn to touch the last Dalek, kept in chains in Henry Van Statten's museum. It is her emotions that then save her when the Dalek escapes, as it cannot bring itself to kill her.

DATA FILE
ORIGIN:
LONDON, ENGLAND

OCCUPATION:
SHOP ASSISTANT, TORCHWOOD AGENT

DOCTORS MET:
9TH, 10TH

SALAMANDER
ENEMY OF THE WORLD

Salamander is a dangerous and cunning inventor and politician. He is a potential world dictator from Mexico who makes natural disasters happen in order to get what he wants. Coincidentally, he looks identical to the Second Doctor.

ASTRID FERRIER

Astrid discovers the Doctor on an Australian beach and rescues him from pursuers in her mini-helicopter. She helps him overthrow the dangerous plans of Salamander. Like everyone else the Doctor meets, she is startled at the resemblance.

STRIKING RESEMBLANCE TO THE SECOND DOCTOR

COPYCATS

The Doctor impersonates Salamander to bring about his downfall, but Salamander also pretends to be the Doctor. He operates the TARDIS controls while the doors are still open and he is ejected into space.

Salamander is popular and considered a saviour. Many people call him "the shopkeeper of the world" because he invented Sun Store, which collects rays from the sun to force-grow crops.

DATA FILE

ORIGIN:
EARTH

SPECIAL ABILITIES:
DICTATING

DOCTORS MET:
2ND

SALLY SPARROW
THE COMPANION THAT NEVER WAS

Sally Sparrow is a photographer who discovers a message written in 1969 by the Doctor to her, with a warning about the Weeping Angels. When her best friend Kathy is zapped into the past by the stone statues, she teams up with Kathy's brother to stop them stealing the TARDIS.

DATA FILE
ORIGIN:
EARTH
SPECIAL ABILITIES:
FIGURING OUT CRYPTIC MESSAGES
DOCTORS MET:
10TH

CLEVER AND COURAGEOUS

WARM COAT FOR NIGHTTIME PHOTOGRAPHY SHOOTS

Sally is bright, brave and a little bit dangerous. She's not put off by keep-out signs, doesn't like to be patronised and is furious that the Angels have taken her friend.

WEEPING ANGELS
It's up to Sally to figure out how to stop the Weeping Angels from getting the TARDIS and return it to the Doctor. She faces them with incredible courage and succeeds in beating them.

"DON'T BLINK"
The Doctor and Martha are stuck in 1969 without the TARDIS. They need Sally to rescue them, but the only way they can communicate is through pre-recorded messages on DVDs.

SARAH JANE SMITH
CLOSE COMPANION

Sarah Jane Smith is one of the Doctor's closest companions. A trained journalist, her curious nature and nose for a good story often gets her into some sticky situations. She fought a host of aliens – Ice Warriors, Daleks, Cybermen and Sontarans – before being left on Earth by the Doctor.

DATA FILE
ORIGIN:
FOXGROVE, ENGLAND

OCCUPATION:
JOURNALIST,
DEFENDER OF EARTH

DOCTORS MET:
1st, 2nd, 3rd, 4th, 5th, 10th, 11th

SCHOOL REUNION
Later in her life, Sarah Jane has an emotional reunion with the Doctor while investigating strange goings-on at a school. She reveals how hurt she has been that he has never returned for her.

STOWAWAY SARAH JANE
Soon after her first meeting with the Doctor, Sarah Jane is determined to investigate the mysterious disappearance of a group of scientists. She stows aboard the TARDIS which takes her back to the Middle Ages where Linx, a Sontaran, is holding the scientists captive.

Sarah Jane continues to fight aliens on Earth with robot dog K-9, super-computer Mr Smith and a team of young investigators. Working from her attic, she bravely takes on all manner of menaces and has helped save the world countless times.

THE SATURNYNS

VAMPIRIC SPACE FISH

The Saturnyns are a race of fish-like aliens that drink blood. When their planet is lost to alien species The Silence, they flee to Earth through a crack in the universe. They establish a new home in 16th century Venice and set about turning it into Saturnyne Mark II.

BLOOD SUCKERS

In their true form, Saturnyns look like a cross between a lobster and a fish. They convert young women into Saturnyns, also known as Sisters of the Water, by draining their blood and replacing it with their own.

Rosanna and Francesco wear perception filters that make them appear human to onlookers. However, they still have vampire-like fangs and their reflections cannot be seen in mirrors.

DATA FILE

HOMEWORLD:
SATURNYNE

SPECIAL ABILITIES:
SHAPE-SHIFTING, CONVERSION

DOCTORS MET:
11TH

SCARECROW SOLDIERS
SERVANTS OF THE FAMILY OF BLOOD

The Scarecrows are the foot soldiers of the Family of Blood, used in their quest to hunt down the Doctor. Stuffed with straw and of limited intelligence, they are the creations of Son of Mine who brought them to life using molecular fringe animation. They are a scary sight as they lurch menacingly towards their victims.

DATA FILE

HOMEWORLD:
CREATED ON EARTH

SPECIAL ABILITIES:
CAN REANIMATE EVEN AFTER SEVERE DAMAGE

DOCTORS MET:
10TH

SCHOOL UNDER SIEGE
With the Doctor in hiding in Farringham School for Boys, the Family order their straw soldiers to attack. The scarecrows are stopped by a hail of bullets, but are later reanimated.

The Scarecrows are instrumental in helping the bodiless Family of Blood find new forms for themselves. They kidnap a farmer, a maid and a schoolgirl, then take them back to the Family's ship to be taken over.

SCAROTH

LAST OF THE JAGAROTH

The Jagaroth was a race of highly advanced, vicious and war-like creatures that existed millions of years ago. When their pilot, Scaroth, tried to leave prehistoric Earth, the Jagaroth spaceship blew up and the race was wiped out, apart from Scaroth. He was splintered into twelve identical bodies that are connected through time.

CHANGING HISTORY
Scaroth wants to go back in time to stop his ship blowing up in order to save his people. The radioactive explosion it creates triggers the start of life on Earth.

Scaroth is a revolting creature with green skin and a single, unblinking eye. For most of his time on Earth, Scaroth chooses to hide his alien features beneath a realistic human mask.

DATA FILE

HOMEWORLD:
PLANET OF THE JAGAROTH RACE

SPECIAL ABILITIES:
HUMAN DISGUISE, TIME TRAVEL, INVENTING, TELEPATHY

DOCTORS MET:
4TH

SEA DEVILS
UNDERWATER MENACE

The Sea Devils are an intelligent race of reptile creatures. Their species are related to the Silurians and are incredibly advanced. They ruled Earth when man was just an ape and have many colonies, each containing thousands of their kind, all over the world.

When Sea Devil astronomers falsely predicted a great catastrophe that would end all life on Earth, the reptilian humanoids hid underground and went into hibernation. Waking up millions of years later, they want to reclaim the planet.

AWAKENING
The Master uses a sonar device to wake a group of Sea Devils hibernating in the English Channel. The Doctor's old enemy wants them to rule Earth again.

POSSIBLE PEACE
The Doctor recognises the Sea Devil race. He tries to persuade them to share the planet with humans and make them live in peace. The Sea Devils consider the possibilty.

DATA FILE
HOMEWORLD:
EARTH
SPECIAL ABILITIES:
SWIMMING, HIBERNATING
DOCTORS MET:
3RD, 5TH

SENSORITES
TELEPATHIC RACE

The Sensorites are a species of advanced and telepathic aliens. A quiet race, they are afraid of what might happen to their planet when Earth discovers them. Sensorites are afraid of the dark and react badly to loud noises. They live near the Ood home planet, Ood-Sphere.

TRAPPED
Wary of outsiders, the Sensorites steal the lock of the TARDIS, briefly trapping the Doctor and his fellow time travellers in the 28th century.

The Sensorite population is endangered by a horrific plague when humans first make contact with them. After this, the Sensorite people are scared of human contact.

DATA FILE

HOMEWORLD:
SENSE-SPHERE

SPECIAL ABILITIES:
TELEPATHY, LOCK PICKING

DOCTORS MET:
1ST

SERGEANT BENTON
ASSOCIATE OF UNIT

Benton is a friendly, down-to-earth member of UNIT who aids the exiled third Doctor in his battles against alien invaders. He is reliably loyal and brave, although he occasionally finds himself outwitted by UNIT's enemies. In such situations, he inevitably finds himself on the receiving end of the Brigadier's exasperated put-downs!

TARDIS TRAVEL
When the first three Doctors unite to fight the insane Omega, Benton gets his first – and only – trip in the TARDIS, finding himself on Omega's desolate anti-matter world.

DATA FILE

ORIGIN:
ENGLAND, EARTH

OCCUPATION:
UNIT SERGEANT

DOCTORS MET:
2ND, 3RD, 4TH

LOYAL TO THE DOCTOR

When he first meets the Doctor, Benton is a Corporal, before being promoted to the rank of Sergeant. Around the time of the Doctor's third regeneration, he becomes a Warrant Officer, but ultimately leaves UNIT to sell second-hand cars.

MILITARY OUTFIT

SHAKRI

PEST CONTROLLERS OF THE UNIVERSE

The Doctor was told about the Shakri as a child but assumed they were a myth to keep young Gallifreyans in their place. The Shakri exist in all of time, serving something called the Tally. They view mankind as pests that must be erased before they colonise space.

CLEVER CUBES
The Shakri send millions of cubes to Earth. They appear to be doing nothing but are actually gathering data on how the Shakri can best wipe out "the human plague".

APPEARS AS HOLOGRAM TO THE DOCTOR

SHAKRI SERVANTS
The Shakri are served by grate-faced orderlies who kidnap humans for experimentation aboard the Shakri sanctum, and an outlier-droid disguised as a human girl.

The Shakri's spacecraft is in orbit one dimension to the left of our universe. It is connected to Earth through seven portals and seven minutes.

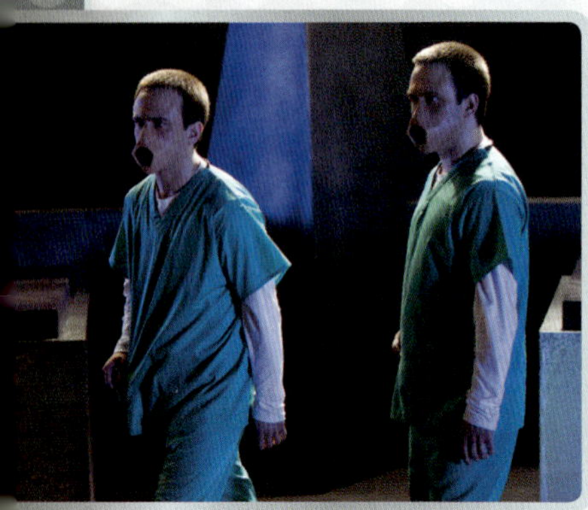

DATA FILE

HOMEWORLD:
UNKNOWN

SPECIAL ABILITIES:
HOLOGRAPHIC PROJECTION, LASER-FIRING

DOCTORS:
11TH

SHARAZ JEK
MASKED ANDROID CREATOR

Sharaz Jek was a doctor before the study of androids took over his life. A brilliant, but slightly mad scientist, he and his business partner, Morgus, settle on planet Androzani Minor, a barren world that contains a highly prized and much fought over substance called spectrox.

DATA FILE

HOMEWORLD: ANDROZANI MINOR

SPECIAL ABILITIES: BUILDING ANDROIDS

DOCTORS MET: 5TH

A mud burst on Androzani Minor results in Jek being horrifically scalded. He wears a leather suit to protect his damaged body, something that even he cannot bear to see.

ANDROID COPIES

A skilful engineer, Jek makes faultless android copies of the Doctor and Peri. Later, he becomes infatuated with the Doctor's companion, who nearly dies from spectrox toxaemia after falling into a spectrox nest.

BENEATH THE MASK

Jek prefers the company of androids because they do not care about his terrible disfigurement. He reveals his face to a shocked Morgus, who later dies.

SIL THE MENTOR
REPTILIAN BUSINESSMAN

Sil is a Mentor from the watery planet Thoros Beta. He looks like a reptilian slug and possesses a vile laugh. Like all Mentors, Sil wants to make lots of money. He is self-obsessed and his favourite food is a local delicacy called marsh minnows.

DATA FILE

HOMEWORLD: THOROS BETA

INTERESTS: BUYING AND DEALING

DOCTORS MET: 6TH

SCHEMING SIL
Sil travels to the planet Varos to negotiate a deal for the Galatron Mining Corporation. He tries to exploit the locals, who do not realise the value of the rare mineral on their planet.

BIG BRAINS
Ruler of the Mentors on Thoros Beta, Lord Kiv's brain is too big for his head. He is in considerable pain until his brain is removed and placed inside the head of Peri, the Doctor's companion.

An unpleasant creature, Sil likes watching humans suffer. He is particularly interested in the various different tortures shown to people on the planet Varos.

THE SILENCE

MEMORY-PROOF HUMANOIDS

These tall, skeletal aliens have the eerie ability to erase themselves from people's memories the instant they look away from them. Worse still, a Silent can easily absorb electricity from their surroundings, which they then unleash from their long fingers, reducing their victims' bodies to burnt fragments in the blink of an eye.

DATA FILE

HOMEWORLD:
UNKNOWN

SPECIAL ABILITIES:
MEMORY ERASURE, POST-HYPNOTIC SUGGESTION

DOCTORS MET:
11TH

The Silence affected humanity's development over thousands of years. They influenced man's decision to go to the moon in 1969. When the Doctor became aware of them, he used the creatures' own powers of post-hypnotic suggestion to turn mankind against them.

TANK TERROR

In an alternate reality, Earth's military forces believe they have succeeded in capturing dozens of the aliens. However, The Silence are only pretending, and easily break out of their water tanks, before electrocuting everyone in sight.

SENTINELS OF HISTORY

The creatures are the leaders of The Silence, a religious movement whose sole purpose is to destroy the Doctor before he can provide the answer to the oldest question in the Universe... Doctor who?

SILURIANS
HOMO REPTILIA

Silurians are a race of reptilian humanoids that ruled Earth millions of years ago. They went into hibernation deep underground when an apocalypse was predicted, but planned to wake once the danger had passed. They believe they are the true owners of Earth and humans are trespassers.

SILURIAN VARIANTS
The Doctor has fought various species of Silurians. The first type he encounters have three eyes, the second have suckers on their fingers, the third have tongues laced with venom.

Silurian society is divided into different classes: warriors, scientists and statesmen. Some believe humans are dumb apes that should be wiped out, while others believe that they can live together in harmony.

DRAGGED DOWN
The Silurians awake from hibernation when a powerful drill threatens the safety of their city. They immediately strike back by dragging humans underground for experimentation.

DATA FILE
ORIGIN:
EARTH
SPECIAL ABILITIES:
ADVANCED SCIENCE, POISONOUS TONGUE, HIBERNATION
DOCTORS MET:
3RD, 5TH, 11TH

SISTERHOOD OF KARN
GUARDIANS OF THE SACRED FLAME

Along with the High Council of Time Lords on Gallifrey, the Sisterhood of Karn also knows the secret of the Elixir of Life. They are responsible for guarding the Sacred Flame that produces the Elixir. The Sisterhood have many powers, including teleportation.

MAREN
High Priestess Maren leads the Sisterhood. She is present at the execution of Morbius on Karn. A strong and old woman, she dies in order to save the Doctor's life.

A group of serious women, the Sisterhood think that the Doctor is trying to steal the last remains of the Elixir from them. As servants of the flame, they fear that if it dies, so will they.

TARDIS THEFT
Using their powers of teleportation and telekinesis, the Sisterhood is able to transport the Doctor's TARDIS into their shrine so that the Doctor is not able to escape the planet.

DATA FILE
HOMEWORLD: KARN
SPECIAL ABILITIES: TELEKINESIS
DOCTORS MET: 4TH

SISTERS OF PLENITUDE
FELINE HUMANOIDS

The Sisters are sinister cat nuns who run the hospital on New Earth in the year 5,000,000,023. They specialise in treating incurable diseases, however the Doctor discovers the Sisters are secretly using humans as lab rats and infecting them with every known disease in the pursuit of developing new cures.

DATA FILE

HOMEWORLD:
NEW EARTH

SPECIAL ABILITIES:
TREATING INCURABLE DISEASES

DOCTORS: MET
10TH

The Matron, Casp, also known as "Whiskers", leads the Sisterhood, which includes Sister Jatt and Sister Corvin. The Catkind nuns worship the goddess Santori.

NOVICE HAME

Novice Hame is a young cat nun whose duty it is to look after the dying Face of Boe. When the Sister's secret is exposed, her penance is to care for him for the rest of their lives, a punishment she accepts with humility.

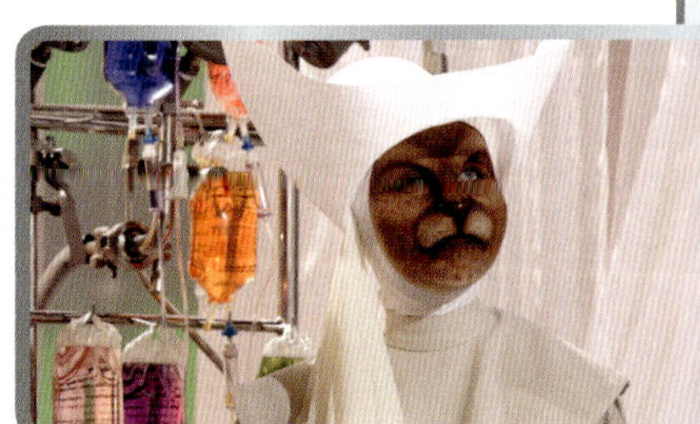

DEADLY DISEASES

When some of the infected humans escape their ward they start passing on diseases to anyone they come into contact with – including Matron Casp, who ends up plummeting to her death!

SLITHEEN

FAMILY OF ALIEN CRIMINALS

Big, green, baby-faced aliens, the Slitheen are notorious criminals from another world. Ruthless and well-organised, they infiltrate the British government by compressing their huge bodies into human skin-suits, enabling them to impersonate MPs. They plan to start a nuclear war and sell off radioactive remnants of Earth as fuel.

SLITHEEN REVEALED
After gathering experts on alien life forms in Downing Street, General Asquith unzips his forehead, revealing the Slitheen under the skinsuit. The Slitheen then electrocute their human captives.

DATA FILE

HOMEWORLD:
RAXACORICOFALLAPATORIUS

SPECIAL ABILITIES:
CAN SHRINK THEMSELVES INTO SKINSUITS

DOCTORS MET:
9TH

The Slitheen have their weaknesses. They can give themselves away by excessive farting, a side effect of the compression process. As calcium-based creatures, they are vulnerable to acetic acid which causes them to explode!

SMILERS
STARSHIP UK ROBOTS

Smilers are frozen-faced robots who work on the *Starship UK*. Some are teachers, others are guards or information points. They protect a dark secret at the heart of the spaceship and their smiles turn to snarls if anyone tries to discover what it is.

DATA FILE
HOMEWORLD: *STARSHIP UK*
SPECIAL ABILITIES: ROTATING HEAD, DISPENSING INFORMATION, KEEPING ORDER
DOCTORS MET: 11TH

The Smilers don't want anyone to know that the *Starship UK* is being carried on the back of a tortured star whale. Anyone who finds out this secret is fed to the captured creature.

WINDERS
Winders look human until their heads rotate to reveal a scary Smiler face on the back. They wear keys, which they use to wind up the Smilers like clocks.

FROZEN SMILES
Some Smilers are stationed in glass booths around *Starship UK*. People are terrified of them. They have the ability to walk out of their booths when necessary.

SOLOMON

VICIOUS SPACE TRADER

Violent and ruthless, Solomon is a space trader who only sees people in terms of their monetary value. He searches for opportunities for profit across the nine galaxies. When a Silurian ark crosses his path, Solomon massacres their crew to get his hands on their precious cargo of dinosaurs.

SCARRED FACE

SPACE-FARING TRADER, PIRATE AND MURDERER

CRIPPLED WHEN RAPTORS CHEWED HIS LEGS

PRECIOUS BOUNTY
Solomon is delighted to learn there is something even more precious than the dinosaurs on board the ark – Queen Nefertiti. He sees her as a bounty that will make him rich.

Solomon is motivated by greed. He wants to sell the dinosaurs on the Roxborne Peninsula, but the ark automatically sets a course for Earth instead and Solomon is powerless to stop it.

DATA FILE

HOMEWORLD:
UNKNOWN

CHARACTER TRAIT:
RUTHLESS GREED

DOCTORS MET:
11TH

SOLOMON'S ROBOTS

METAL TANTRUM MACHINES

The space trader Solomon bought these robots at a discount from a concession on Illyria Seven. After two millennia, their bodies are falling apart and rusty. By nature, they are irritable and often snap at each other, but are perfect for Solomon's needs.

The robots follow Solomon's orders without question. They try to repair him when he is attacked by raptors, they murder the Silurians and they shoot Brian. They have no moral code.

TOO SLOW

Acting as Solomon's henchmen, the robots frogmarch the Doctor, Brian and Rory to their leader. But because of their bulk and age, the robots are not as fast as they used to be. When their captives gallop away on a triceratops, they can't keep up.

DATA FILE

HOMEWORLD: ILLYRIA SEVEN

SPECIAL ABILITIES: FIRING LASER-BOLTS

DOCTORS MET: 11TH

SONTARAN
CLONE WARRIORS

Sontarans are a vicious clone race from the planet Sontar. The Eleventh Doctor describes them as "psychotic potato-faced dwarfs". Sontarans live for the honour of battle and have been locked in war with their enemies, the Rutans, for thousands of years.

BATTLE CRY IS "SONTAR-HA!"

SHORT, STOCKY AND STRONG

BODY WEIGHS SEVERAL TONNES ON HIGH GRAVITY SONTAR

DATA FILE

HOMEWORLD:
SONTAR

SPECIAL ABILITIES:
CLONING THEMSELVES, MILITARY TACTICS AND WARFARE

DOCTORS MET:
2nd, 3rd, 4th, 6th, 10th, 11th

Entire legions of Sontaran clones are produced together in factories on Sontar. As a result, they all look similar, though they are assigned different ranks.

NURSE STRAX
Strax suffers the greatest humiliation a Sontaran can endure – he is forced to become a nurse. He aids the Doctor on Demon's Run and also helps him fight the Great Intelligence alongside Madame Vastra and Jenny.

SONTAR-HA!
In the Middle Ages, a Sontaran called Linx tries to claim Earth for his own. Sontarans also attempt to invade Gallifrey and to turn Earth into a clone world.

STEVEN TAYLOR
PILOT COMPANION

Spaceship pilot Steven is captured by the robotic Mechonoids after crashlanding on their planet. The robots keep him prisoner for two years until the Doctor and his friends arrive and help him to escape. Amid a war between Daleks and Mechonoids, Steven barely escapes with his life, and ends up stumbling aboard the TARDIS.

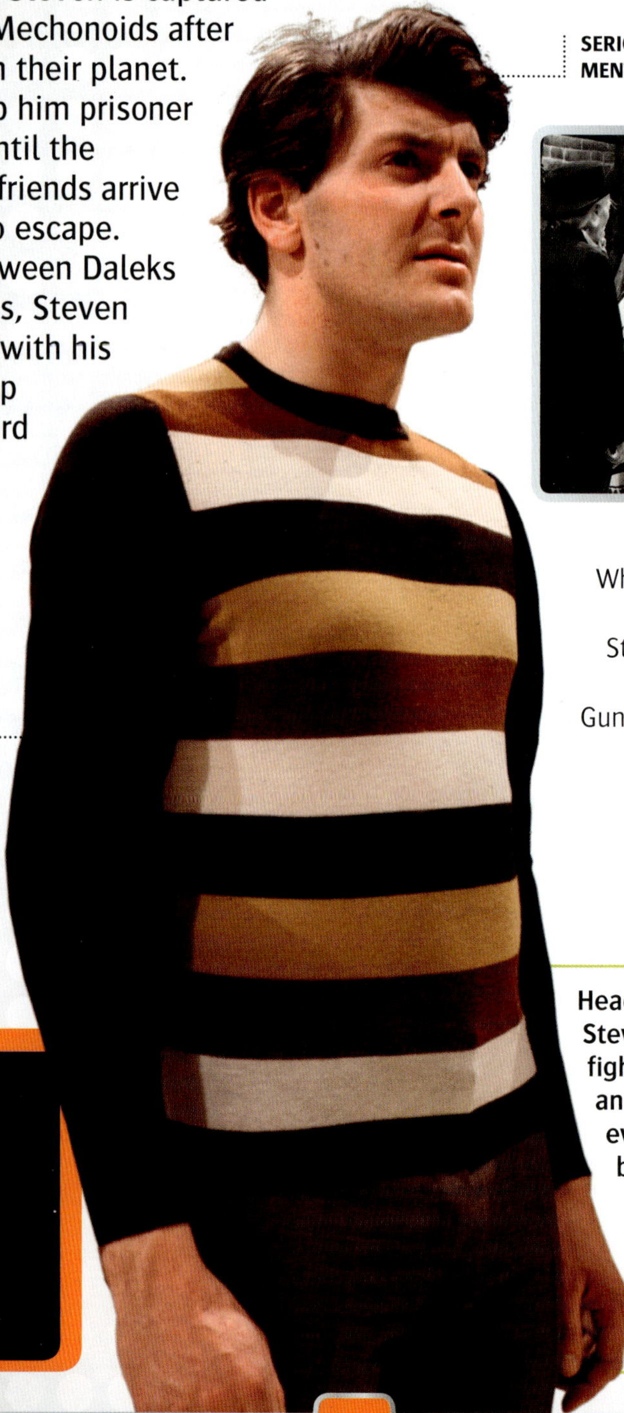

SERIOUS MENTALITY

FITTED JUMPER FOR EASE OF MOVEMENT IN SPACESHIP

THE WILD, WILD WEST
When the TARDIS materialises in the Wild West in 1881, Steven is caught up in events leading to the infamous Gunfight at the OK Corral – and is almost lynched by the outlaw Clanton family!

Headstrong and courageous, Steven helps the Doctor fight against the Daleks and Drahvins, but eventually leaves to help build a new society on an alien world, uniting the technologically advanced Elders and the planet's savage inhabitants.

DATA FILE
ORIGIN:
EARTH
OCCUPATION:
ASTRONAUT
DOCTORS MET:
1st

SUSAN FOREMAN
THE DOCTOR'S GRANDDAUGHTER

A lively young teenager, Susan is the Doctor's very first travelling companion and also his granddaughter. She is curious about ordinary life on Earth and persuades her grandfather to allow her to attend Coal Hill School in 1960s London. However, her levels of knowledge are so unbalanced that her schoolteachers soon become suspicious of her.

SUSAN AND THE SENSORITES
When the Doctor and his friends encounter a timid race called the Sensorites, Susan discovers she is able to use her powers of telepathy to communicate with the creatures.

DATA FILE

ORIGIN:
GALLIFREY

SPECIAL ABILITIES:
TELEPATHY

DOCTORS MET:
1st, 2nd, 3rd, 5th

STRIPED TUNIC

LOOKS LIKE A TEENAGER THOUGH HER TIME LORD GENES MEAN SHE IS LIKELY TO BE OLDER

After helping to defeat the Daleks, Susan falls in love with resistance fighter David Campbell. She's upset to leave her grandfather, but the Doctor locks her out of the ship and she remains on Earth to begin a new life.

SUTEKH THE DESTROYER
LAST OF THE OSIRIANS

An ancient and dangerous Osirian, Sutekh the Destroyer longs for the destruction of all living things. Beneath his mask lies the horrific face of a jackal. He is responsible for the destruction of his own planet and is now the very last of his kind.

Trapped beneath an Egyptian pyramid by his brother, Sutekh goes undiscovered for 7,000 years. A British archaeologist eventually opens his tomb and nearly brings about the destruction of all mankind.

PYRAMID POWER
Sutekh uses the strong, silent Osirian robot mummies to aid his escape from imprisonment. He then instructs the building of a rocket designed to destroy the controls that hold him captive, but the Doctor and Sarah Jane manage to stop him.

DATA FILE

HOMEWORLD:
PHAESTER OSIRIS

SPECIAL ABILITIES:
SPACE TRAVEL, PATIENCE, MIND CONTROL

DOCTORS MET:
4TH

SYCORAX
HUMANOID SCAVENGERS

The Sycorax are a race of savage, war-like scavengers who roam the universe ransacking planets of their resources and enslaving their inhabitants. On Christmas Day 2006, one of their asteroid spaceships approaches Earth and the Sycorax use blood control to possess a third of its population, ordering the world to surrender.

The Sycorax wear scary bone helmets which both hide and protect an even more terrifying sight beneath. The creatures appear to have no outer skin, their faces made up of only bone and muscle.

DUELLING THE DOCTOR
The Doctor challenges the Sycorax leader to a sword fight. He wins the duel and spares the Sycorax's life, on the condition that his people leave the planet and never return.

DATA FILE

HOMEWORLD:
UNKNOWN

SPECIAL ABILITIES:
HYPNOSIS BY BLOOD CONTROL

DOCTORS MET:
10TH

SYLVIA NOBLE
DONNA NOBLE'S MOTHER

Sharp-tongued Sylvia Noble is mother to Donna, wife to Geoff and daughter to Wilfred Mott. She is often critical of her daughter but will snap at anyone else who dares say a word against her. Ever since the Doctor's arrival in Donna's life, Sylvia has been terrified on her behalf.

MOTHER OF THE BRIDE
When Donna vanishes on her wedding day, Sylvia thinks it is one of her "silly little look-at-me party pieces", then panics that she may be dead. However, all is happily resolved when, a few years later, Donna marries the man of her dreams.

TROUBLE MAKER
In Sylvia's mind, whenever the Doctor appears, disaster follows – such as the time Daleks arrive on her doorstep. She blames the Doctor for ruining Donna's wedding and disapproves of her father Wilfred's friendship with him.

DATA FILE
ORIGIN: EARTH
SPECIAL ABILITIES: TELLING PEOPLE OFF
DOCTORS MET: 10TH

Sylvia is amazed to learn her daughter is travelling the stars. And when the Doctor is forced to wipe Donna's mind of their adventures, Sylvia proudly defends her.

TARDIS

THE DOCTOR'S AMAZING BLUE BOX

The TARDIS is a space-time machine used by Time Lords. The Doctor could once change its exterior to match its surroundings, but a fault means its shell is stuck as a 1950s police box. Inside, it has ever-changing console rooms. It is dimensionally transcendental so is far bigger on the inside than it looks.

DATA FILE

HOMEWORLD: GALLIFREY

SPECIAL ABILITIES: BEING BIGGER ON THE INSIDE, FLYING THROUGH SPACE AND TIME, TRANSLATING ALIEN LANGUAGES

DOCTORS MET: ALL

HUMAN FORM

When the TARDIS takes human form, she reveals that she doesn't always take the Doctor where he wants to go, but she always takes him where he needs to be.

The TARDIS was once powered by a black hole called the Eye of Harmony. Now it refuels using temporal radiation from the Rift. The Doctor can energise it with his life force, too.

TEGAN JOVANKA
ACCIDENTAL COMPANION

A brash and bossy Australian air stewardess, Tegan becomes a traveller in the TARDIS quite by accident, thinking it is a real police box. At first, she is desperate to get back to Heathrow airport, but as time goes by, she comes to accept her new life as the Doctor's companion, even witnessing his regeneration into the Fifth Doctor.

MOUTH ON LEGS

Tegan doesn't suffer fools gladly and her short temper means she often gets into arguments with the Doctor. At one point, she admits her faults, describing herself as "just a mouth on legs"!

SMART AIR STEWARDESS HAIRCUT

BRIGHT 1980s PATTERN

PARTYING WITH ALIENS

Aboard one of the Eternal's sailing ships, Tegan gets a rare chance to dress up. However, she doesn't realise one of the creatures intends to plant an explosive device on her!

During her travels, Tegan ends up fighting everything from Sea Devils and Silurians to Terileptils and Tractators. Sadly, during an encounter with the Daleks, Tegan is overcome by all the deaths she has witnessed and decides to leave the Doctor.

DATA FILE

ORIGIN:
BRISBANE, AUSTRALIA

OCCUPATION:
AIR STEWARDESS

DOCTORS MET:
1st, 2nd, 3rd, 4th, 5th

TERILEPTIL
REPTILIAN CRIMINALS

Terileptils are an intelligent and advanced race of reptile creatures. They love art and beauty, but also love war. They enjoy fighting and believe war is honourable. If convicted, criminal Terileptils are sentenced to life imprisonment, working in the tinclavic mines of the planet Raaga.

DATA FILE

HOMEWORLD: UNKNOWN

SPECIAL ABILITIES: STRENGTH, CREATING ANDROIDS, MIND CONTROL

DOCTORS MET: 5TH

ANDROIDS
Terileptils use beautifully designed androids to carry out different tasks. On Earth, an android disguises itself as the Grim Reaper to scare the primitive locals it encounters.

In the middle of the 1600s, a group of Terileptil prisoners escape Raaga and become stranded on Earth. Unable to go home, they plan to rid Earth of human life and claim the planet for themselves. However, they die in a fire, which also destroys a large part of London in 1666.

TESELECTA

JUSTICE DEPARTMENT VEHICLE

The *Teselecta* is a highly advanced, humanoid shape-changing time-space machine from the future. The *Teselecta*'s function is to track down criminals who escaped unpunished during their lives and administer its own justice in the form of torture.

INSIDE THE *TESELECTA*
The *Teselecta* is manned by a crew that has been reduced in size by a compression field.

The *Teselecta* can take the shape of any creature it has scanned. At one point, it even copies a Nazi official in its attempt to bring Adolf Hitler to justice.

CHEATING DEATH
In 2011, the *Teselecta*'s Captain agrees to help the Doctor cheat death. Copying his form, the *Teselecta* is repeatedly shot by a mysterious astronaut, while the real Doctor remains safe inside it.

TESELECTA CAPTAIN CARTER

DATA FILE

HOMEWORLD:
UNKNOWN

SPECIAL ABILITIES:
SHAPE-SHIFTING, INTERNAL COMPRESSION FIELD

DOCTORS MET:
11TH

THALS
PEACEFUL RACE

The Thals come from the planet Skaro, also home of the much-feared Daleks. Thousands of years ago they were at war with the Kaleds – the race that eventually mutated into the Daleks. After a destructive war on their shared home planet, Thals change their ways and become peaceful.

FIGHTING DALEKS
In order to survive mass extermination, the Thal people have to learn to fight the Daleks again. It is against all their principles, but without a fight they will become extinct.

Beautiful humanoids, Thals tend to have blonde hair and fair skin. They take anti-radiation drugs to survive the effects of the nuclear war between them and the Daleks.

ALYDON, LEADER OF THE THALS

UNEVEN MATCH
A group of Thals goes to the planet Spiridon to help stop the Daleks. They discover that the Daleks have a hidden army of 10,000.

DATA FILE
HOMEWORLD:
SKARO

SPECIAL ABILITIES:
LOGIC, FARMING

DOCTORS MET:
1st, 3rd, 4th

TOBIAS VAUGHN
CYBERMAN COLLABORATOR

Cold, calm and incredibly powerful, Tobias Vaughn is the charming managing director of International Electromatics, a large electronics company. His body is part converted by the Cybermen, whom he helps to invade Earth.

POWER TRIP
Vaughn is using the Cybermen as much as they are using him. He wants to rule Earth, but the Doctor persuades him to help defeat the Cybermen. He is killed while helping to stop the invasion.

An almost inhuman character, Vaughn hardly ever blinks. The normal range of human blinking is about once every ten or 15 seconds, but Vaughn blinks far less frequently.

INVASION
Vaughn is unaware that the Cybermen intend to destroy all human life after their invasion of Earth, and turns against them when he discovers this.

DATA FILE
ORIGIN: EARTH
SPECIAL ABILITIES: LEADING INVASIONS
DOCTORS MET: 2ND

TOCLAFANE
LAST EVOLUTION OF HUMANITY

At first sight, the Toclafane appear to be hovering robotic spheres, armed with deadly energy beams and razor-sharp knives. Inside each casing, however, is a shrivelled, disembodied human head, for the Toclafane are what the human race will become in order to survive trillions of years in the future.

The Master names the Toclafane after a character from a Gallifreyan fairy tale. The creatures speak in childish sing-song voices, share a collective memory and appear to have regressed to a primitive level, enjoying killing for its own sake.

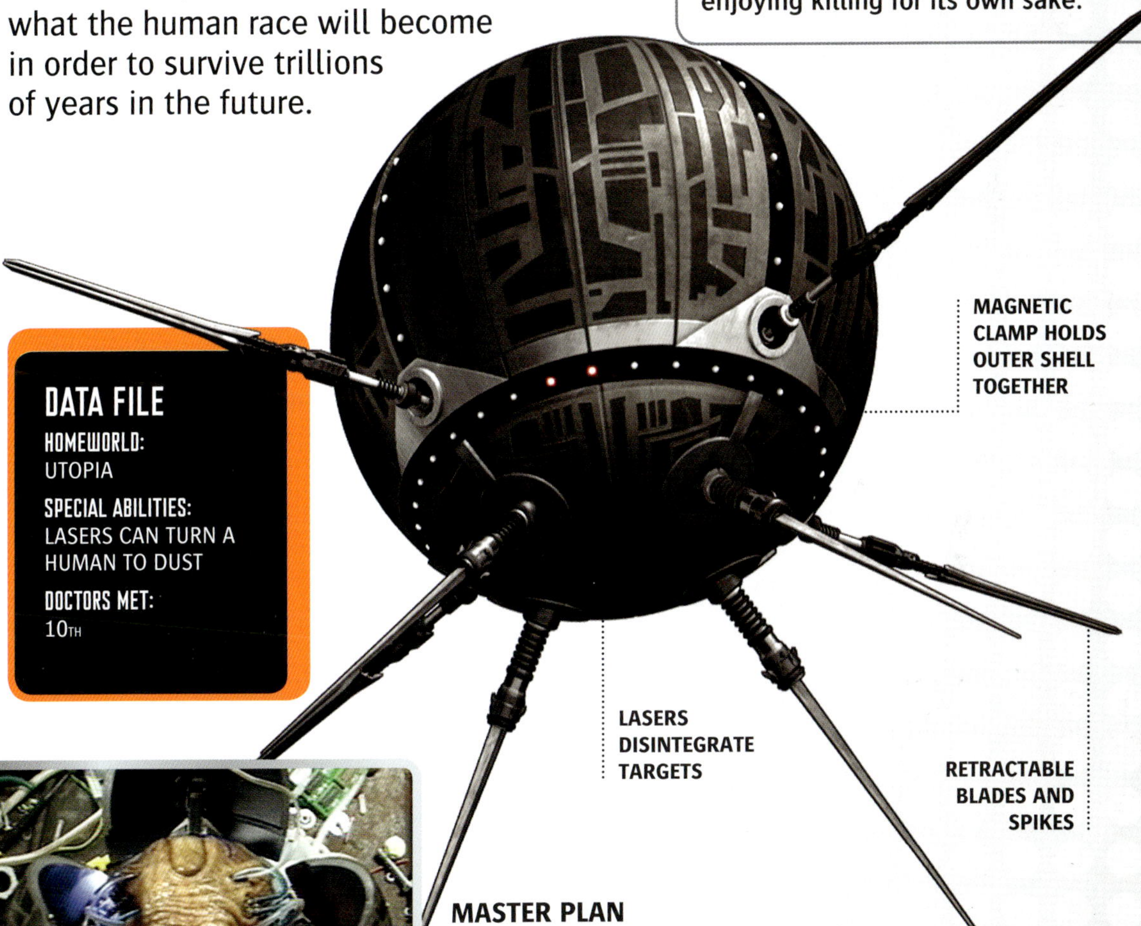

DATA FILE

HOMEWORLD:
UTOPIA

SPECIAL ABILITIES:
LASERS CAN TURN A HUMAN TO DUST

DOCTORS MET:
10TH

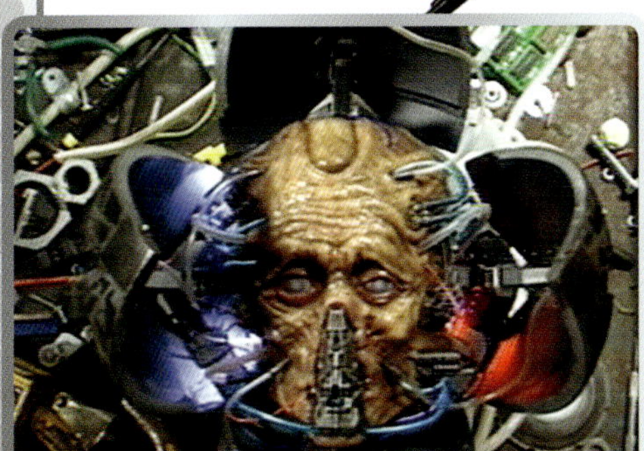

MASTER PLAN

Using the Doctor's TARDIS to power a paradox machine, the Master is able to bring the Toclafane back through time. Billions of them descend to Earth and begin slaughtering their ancestors.

VALEYARD
TIME LORD PROSECUTOR

The word Valeyard means "learned court prosecutor". The Valeyard is an arrogant and angry figure with a dangerous mind, who believes that the Sixth Doctor has broken one of the Laws of Time – and become involved in the affairs of different people and planets.

The Valeyard puts the Doctor on trial and presents evidence from his past, present and future. To begin with, he appears to be working for the High Council of Time Lords. However, he is eventually exposed as being an amalgamation of the darker sides of the Doctor's nature.

TIME LORD ON TRIAL
The Valeyard brings his case against the Doctor before the Inquisitor, aboard a massive Time Lord space station. The TARDIS is taken out of time and space as the Doctor fights for his life.

MR POPPLEWICK
The Valeyard uses a disguise to fool the Doctor inside the Time Lord Matrix. Mr Popplewick comes across as a helpful, kindly man who works at J. J. Chamber's Fantasy Factory.

DATA FILE
HOMEWORLD:
GALLIFREY

SPECIAL ABILITIES:
MASTER OF DISGUISE, FAKING EVIDENCE

DOCTORS MET:
6TH

VASHTA NERADA
FLESH-EATING MICRO-ORGANISMS

Known as "the shadows that eat the flesh", the Vashta Nerada are swarms of tiny creatures that can live in any patch of darkness. They are found on most inhabited worlds and are normally content to live on road kill, but they can strip a person's flesh from his bones almost instantaneously.

DATA FILE

ORIGIN:
UNKNOWN

SPECIAL ABILITIES:
STRIPPING FLESH IN AN INSTANT

DOCTORS MET:
10TH

The Vashta Nerada can hatch from the spores in trees, or even from microspores in paper. When they hunt, they latch on to a food source and keep it fresh, mimicking the shadow cast by their prey.

SWARM IN A SPACESUIT
On a vast library world, the Doctor encounters an infestation of Vashta Nerada who devour the flesh of a man in a spacesuit. The swarm then makes his skeleton pursue yet more victims.

SKELETON ATTACK
The Vashta Nerada start reducing people to skeletal zombies one by one, but even when he's caught, the Doctor somehow manages to avoid being eaten alive!

VERVOIDS
DEADLY PLANT LIFE FORMS

The Vervoids are intelligent and deadly. Created by three scientists who planned to sell them on to use as slave labour in farms and factories on Earth, a malfunction in their DNA turned the creatures into dangerous killers wanting to wipe out all of animal-kind.

DATA FILE
HOMEWORLD:
CREATED ON MOGAR
SPECIAL ABILITIES:
KILLING
DOCTORS MET:
6TH

Vervoids need only sunlight and water to survive. Although they have a short lifespan, just one leaf placed in soil is able to create another creature. They are completely destroyed by the Doctor before they reach Earth.

POD SHOCK
When their large green pods are hit with high intensity light, the Vervoids are unleashed aboard a passenger spaceship where they start to kill the crew and passengers.

VESPIFORM

GIANT ALIEN WASPS

The Vespiform are no ordinary wasps! They are 8 foot tall monsters, armed with lethal stingers and the ability to shape-shift. Their hives are in the Silfrax galaxy, but the Doctor and Donna discover a half-human, half-Vespiform vicar murdering people in the style of a Whodunnit novel in 1920s England.

GIANT WINGS FOR FAST FLYING

SUPER-SIZED STINGER

VESPIFORM IN NATURAL RATHER, THAN HUMAN, FORM

Not all Vespiform are bad. One came to Earth and took the form of a man to learn about humankind. He was lost in the Delhi flood in 1885, but left behind him a son. Reverend Golightly has no idea he is part Vespiform until thieves try to steal the church silver and his rage breaks the genetic lock keeping him human.

THE FIRESTONE

The Doctor, with the investigative help of Donna and Agatha Christie, discover that the Vespiform's essence is kept in a telepathic recorder called the Firestone – hidden inside a heart-shaped necklace. It beams the Reverend's true identity directly into his brain.

DATA FILE

HOMEWORLD:
SILFRAX GALAXY

SPECIAL ABILITIES:
SHAPE-CHANGING, FLYING, STINGING

DOCTORS MET:
10TH

VICKI
ADVENTUROUS COMPANION

Vicki is a young teenager whom the Doctor meets on the planet Dido in the 25th century. She is desperately awaiting rescue after the ship she was travelling in crash-landed on the planet. With her mother already dead, she believes the planet's natives have killed her father and most of the ship's crew.

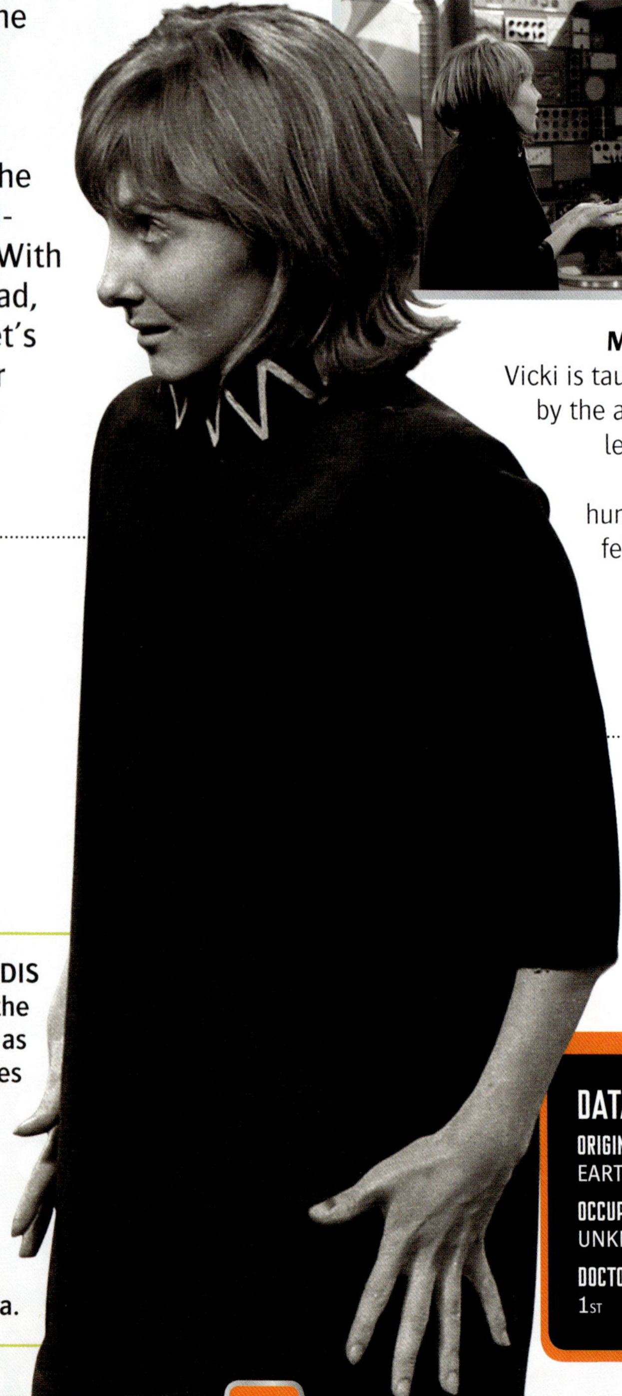

MONSTER MENACE
Vicki is taunted and terrorised by the alien Koquillion, but learns the creature is really Bennett, the human murderer of his fellow crewmembers. He has disguised himself to conceal his guilt.

GOOD ANALYTICAL AND TECHNICAL SKILLS

KEEN FOR ADVENTURE

After joining the TARDIS crew, Vicki encounters the Zarbi and the Drahvins, as well as historical figures such as Emperor Nero and King Richard the Lionheart. She ends up falling in love with Troilus in ancient Troy and adopts a new name: Cressida.

DATA FILE
ORIGIN:
EARTH
OCCUPATION:
UNKNOWN
DOCTORS MET:
1ST

VICTORIA WATERFIELD
BRAVE COMPANION

A modest young girl from the year 1866, Victoria is orphaned when her scientist father Edward Waterfield is killed by the invading Daleks. The Doctor takes her with him in the TARDIS and although Victoria isn't the most willing of adventurers, she overcomes her timidity to stand up to a succession of alien aggressors.

TRADITIONAL VICTORIAN FULL-LENGTH DRESS REPLACED BY MORE PRACTICAL CLOTHES

DALEKS' HOSTAGE
Victoria's father had been experimenting with time travel using mirrors and static electricity. He accidentally linked up with the Daleks and they took Victoria hostage on Skaro.

DATA FILE

ORIGIN:
ENGLAND, EARTH

OCCUPATION:
UNKNOWN

DOCTORS MET:
2ND

STAY CLOSE
The second Doctor's other companion, Jamie McCrimmon, often protects Victoria and rather likes her. Jamie tries in vain to persuade her to stay with him and the Doctor.

During Victoria's travels, she visits the Cyber tombs of Telos and has two terrifying encounters with the Yeti. After destroying a seaweed creature with her amplified screams, she finally tires of being scared and decides to stay on Earth.

VINVOCCI

SPIKY, GREEN HUMANOIDS

Resembling the smaller, red-coloured Zocci, the Vinvocci are a technologically advanced species. In December 2009, two of their kind arrive on Earth and pose as human scientists Rossiter and Addams. Their goal is to retrieve the Immortality Gate – a Vinvocci medical device that can be used to heal the population of entire worlds.

DODGING MISSILES
Rossiter and Addams end up helping the Doctor and Wilfred Mott escape the Master. They fly them back to Earth in their salvaged spaceship, the *Hesperus*, somehow managing to dodge the Master's all-out missile attack.

As well as possessing teleportation technology, the Vinvocci have advanced devices called "Shimmers" which enable them to appear human, although they are very uncomfortable to use. The Shimmers are worn at the wrist, disguised as wristwatches.

DATA FILE

ORIGIN:
UNKNOWN

SPECIAL ABILITIES:
SHAPE-CHANGING TECHNOLOGY

DOCTORS MET:
10TH

VISLOR TURLOUGH
ALIEN COMPANION

An alien from Trion, Vislor Turlough is exiled from his home planet in the aftermath of a civil war. He ends up at an English public school on Earth where he is recruited by the Black Guardian to destroy the Doctor. Regarded by some as shifty and untrustworthy, he succeeds in gaining the Doctor's trust.

Turlough finds it harder than he thought he would to kill the Doctor, realising that the Doctor is a good man. He struggles to live under the shadow of the Black Guardian's promise that he will never be free until his mission is completed.

TAUNTING TURLOUGH
The Black Guardian is furious with Turlough's continued inability to kill the Doctor. In order to rid himself of his tormentor, Turlough throws an immensely powerful diamond at him and the Black Guardian is instantly consumed by flames.

RETURNING TO TRION
Free from the Black Guardian, Turlough is able to travel with the Doctor without fear. Eventually, though, he learns that there's been a change of regime on Trion, and takes the opportunity to return home as a free man.

DATA FILE

HOMEWORLD:
TRION

OCCUPATION:
PUPIL AT A PUBLIC SCHOOL

DOCTORS MET:
1st, 2nd, 3rd, 5th

VOC ROBOTS
ROBOTIC SERVANTS

The Voc Robots are beautiful, elegant creations found on board the Sandminer. They are programmed to carry out the crew's every command from providing refreshments to locating things for them. Usually reliable and unquestioning, the crew are appalled to discover the robots start to disobey and, worse, start to murder crew-members.

TAREN CAPEL
Taren Capel reprograms the robots on board the Sandminer to kill. He has lived with robots from childhood, and now he wants to free his brothers and let them rule the world.

Incredibly strong, robots like this are programmed to obey and never kill. Their design is deliberately humanoid and they have a pleasant, calming and attractive voice.

DATA FILE
ORIGIN:
KALDOR CITY

SPECIAL ABILITIES:
STRENGTH

DOCTORS MET:
4TH

WAR MACHINE
WOTAN'S ARMY

The War Machines are the giant army of tank-like robots created by a super-computer called WOTAN in London's Post Office Tower in 1966. Big, destructive and powerful, they are used by WOTAN in an attempt to take over the world.

WOTAN
WOTAN stands for Will Operating Thought ANalogue. The computer hypnotises its creator, Professor Brett, along with several others, in an attempt to conquer Earth, but is eventually destroyed by one of its own War Machines.

DATA FILE
ORIGIN:
EARTH
SPECIAL ABILITIES:
HYPNOSIS
DOCTORS MET:
1st

Built in a warehouse in London by humans hypnotised by WOTAN, each War Machine has a different number on it, deadly weapons attached to its frame and appears unstoppable.

WEEPING ANGELS
THE LONELY ASSASSINS

One of the deadliest predators in the galaxy, Weeping Angels are an ancient race of stone statues. They are protected by the ultimate defence mechanism – a quantum lock – and can only move when they aren't being observed.

CHERUB ANGELS
The Angels have fought the Doctor three times. They have sent him back to 1969 without his TARDIS and formed an army within an Aplan temple. In their third encounter, the Angels took over New York, aided by mean-spirited Cherub Angels.

Weeping Angels feed off temporal energy, zapping their victims back into the past and consuming the energy from the years they would have lived. Without food, they starve and crumble.

DATA FILE

HOMEWORLD:
UNKNOWN

SPECIAL ABILITIES:
QUANTUM LOCKED, LIGHTNING SPEED, EXTREME STRENGTH

DOCTORS:
10TH, 11TH

WENG-CHIANG
TIME TRAVELLER'S DISGUISE

Weng-Chiang is the name assumed by a dangerous criminal from the 51st century: Magnus Greel. Greel impersonates the Chinese god Weng-Chiang when he becomes stranded in the 19th century and his body is terribly disfigured by being transported back in time.

DATA FILE

ORIGIN:
EARTH

SPECIAL ABILITIES:
TIME TRAVEL

DOCTORS MET:
4TH

MR SIN
Greel travels back in time with a Peking Homunculus cyborg known as Mr Sin. Mr Sin looks like a ventriloquist's dummy but underneath he is a lethal, murderous creature, with the brain of a pig.

The extent of the damage to Greel's body is life-threatening, so he drains the energy of young women in Victorian London to keep himself alive. His arrival also has other dangerous side effects – Zygma energy from Greel's machine enlarges creatures. As a result, giant rats are soon roaming the sewers under London.

WEREWOLF

LUPINE-WAVELENGTH HAEMOVARIFORM

In reality, the Werewolf is a ferocious, shape-changing alien that crashed to Earth and landed in Scotland in 1540. The creature survives by infecting a succession of human hosts, and hundreds of years later it attempts to bite and possess Queen Victoria, aiming to establish its own empire on Earth.

ATTACKING THE QUEEN

Upon the arrival of Queen Victoria and the Doctor at Torchwood House, the alien shape-changer switches from human to its true lupine form and goes on a murderous rampage. Luckily, the Doctor manages to destroy the beast with a beam of focused moonlight.

For all its power, the Werewolf has a weakness – a strange fear of mistletoe. When the Doctor and his friends hide in the library of Torchwood House, the creature refuses to attack, sensing the presence of mistletoe oil in the room's wooden panelling.

DATA FILE

ORIGIN:
UNKNOWN

SPECIAL ABILITIES:
SHAPE-CHANGING, MIGRATION TO NEW HOSTS

DOCTORS MET:
10TH

WILFRED MOTT

GRANDFATHER OF DONNA NOBLE

A wise and gentle old man, Wilf was greatly upset when the Doctor was forced to erase his granddaughter Donna's memories and end her travels. He searched hard to find the Doctor once more, hoping that her condition could be reversed, and ended up joining the Tenth Doctor on his last perilous adventure.

PARACHUTE REGIMENT BADGE FROM DAYS IN NATIONAL SERVICE

AMATEUR ASTRONOMER WITH INTEREST IN ALIEN THEORIES

PRACTICAL OVERCOAT

WARM CLOTHES FOR COLD WINTER WEATHER AND LATE NIGHT STARGAZING

DATA FILE

ORIGIN:
LONDON, ENGLAND

OCCUPATION:
RETIRED SOLDIER, NEWSPAPER SELLER

DOCTORS MET:
10TH

A soldier in his younger days, Wilf's heroic qualities never left him. He bravely helped to defend the Vinvocci ship *Hesperus* against the Master's missile attack, fearlessly manning the ship's laser cannons until the last missile had been destroyed.

THE DOCTOR'S SACRIFICE
When Wilf becomes trapped in a control booth, the only way for the Doctor to free him was to swap places with him, resulting in him absorbing a massive dose of radiation – enough to force him to regenerate.

WIRRN
GIANT INSECTOIDS

The Wirrn are large, intelligent, telepathic insect creatures. They live in space, but when they are hungry they will track down a food source on a planet and also find somewhere to breed. They are able to absorb knowledge from creatures and can live for years without fresh oxygen.

DATA FILE

HOMEWORLD: THE ANDROMEDA GALAXY

SPECIAL ABILITIES: TELEPATHY

DOCTORS MET: 4TH

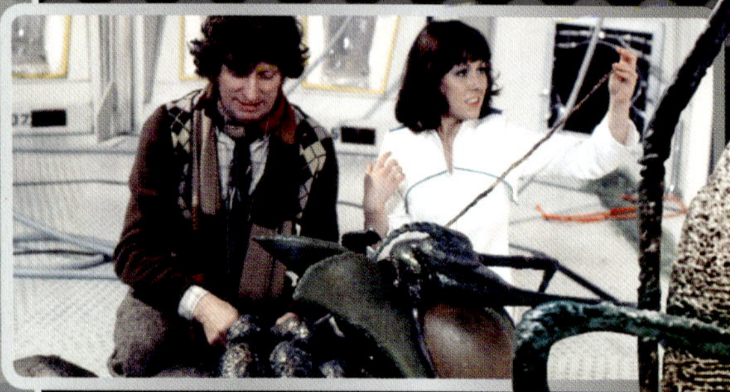

LAYING EGGS

Like a type of wasp that paralyses caterpillars and lays eggs, the Wirrn lay their eggs inside creatures and then have a ready-made food supply when the eggs hatch.

For a thousand years, the Wirrn fought humans until they destroyed their breeding colonies. The Wirrn now drift through space looking for new places to live.

WOODLAND KING AND QUEEN
ANDROZANI TREE ROYALTY

The King and Queen of the Androzani trees are wooden aliens who live on Tree Farm 457 in the year 5345. Their bark is an excellent source of fuel. When harvesters threaten to melt the forest with acid rain for battery fluid, the King and Queen resolve to evacuate their people.

DATA FILE

HOMEWORLD:
TREE FARM 457

SPECIAL ABILITIES:
FAST GROWING, CAN TRANSMUTE INTO A SUB-ETHERIC WAVEBAND OF LIGHT

DOCTORS MET:
11TH

Although they look scary, the King and Queen are harmless. They believe the Doctor's arrival was foretold and have faith that he will save the forest from the acid rain.

HATCHED!
The Wooden King hatches from a silver tree bauble and grows to full size in less than an hour. But his body is just a vessel for the pure life force inside.

THE MOTHERSHIP
The Queen's crown is a relay. By placing it on Madge Arwell, the souls of all the trees zoom into her head and she flies them through the Vortex to safety.

YETI

MASSIVE ROBOTS

The Yeti are massive furry robots that are first mistaken for the Abominable Snowmen in the Himalayas. They are controlled by the Great Intelligence with silver spheres placed inside their chests. Without the sphere, the Yeti robot is powerless.

CAN PRODUCE HORRIFIC ROAR

CONTAINS A SPHERE THAT POWERS ROBOT

CLAWS

BULKY BODY

DATA FILE

HOMEWORLD: CREATED ON EARTH

SPECIAL ABILITIES: STRENGTH

DOCTORS MET: 2ND

WEB OF FEAR

In one invasion attempt, the Yeti storm into London through the Underground transport system and use a dangerous web to engulf and cripple things.

The Great Intelligence – a powerful being from another dimension that can survive without physical form – uses the Yeti in its attempts to take over Earth.

ZARBI
LARGE INSECTOIDS

The Zarbi are large ant-like creatures from the planet Vortis. Normally docile, the Zarbi become menacing when they are taken over by a parasite called the Animus. They are able to control people with a special metal device and also use Vortis Venom Grubs as weapons. Irrationally, they are frightened of spiders.

DATA FILE
HOMEWORLD:
VORTIS
SPECIAL ABILITIES:
STRENGTH, ABLE TO CONTROL OTHERS
DOCTORS: MET
1st

The Zarbi creatures are not an intelligent life form, but were essential to the life pattern on Vortis. The Animus made them too strong for the other inhabitants on the planet.

MENOPTERA
The Animus parasite causes a war between the Zarbi and the Menoptera, a race of butterfly aliens from Vortis. When the Animus is destroyed, the two races co-exist in peace again.

ZOE HERRIOT

SUPER SCIENTIST COMPANION

Zoe is a brilliant astrophysicist who meets the Second Doctor during the Cyberman invasion of the gigantic space-station, the Wheel. After helping him defeat the cyborgs, she decides to stow away in the TARDIS. She soon realises that there's more to life than logic and mathematics and learns much from her experiences with the Doctor.

CYBER PLOT

When Zoe intercepts the invading Cybermen's signals, she learns that the silver cyborgs are planning to trap and kill the Doctor. With her new friend, Jamie, she is determined to find a way to warn him of the danger.

LOGICAL MIND

SAYING GOODBYE

Zoe travels with the Doctor alongside Jamie McCrimmon. And just like Jamie, when the pair leave the TARDIS, Zoe has her memory wiped of all her travels – excluding her very first encounter with the Time Lord.

DATA FILE

ORIGIN:
EARTH

OCCUPATION:
LIBRARIAN, ASTROPHYSICIST

DOCTORS MET:
2ND

Amongst her many adventures, Zoe battles the Cybermen, and encounters the Krotons and Ice Warriors, before she is forced to leave the Doctor by the Time Lords. She returns to the Wheel, while the Doctor is exiled to Earth.

ZYGONS

SHAPE-SHIFTING ALIENS

The powerful Zygons come from a planet that was destroyed centuries ago. A small group of the creatures escape and their ship crashes into Loch Ness, Scotland, where it remains undetected for hundreds of years. Their leader, Broton, wants to make Earth the new Zygon homeworld.

BODY DOUBLES
Zygon technology allows them to take on the appearance of other beings. By keeping the original alive, this horrifying alien shape can change into any creature it captures.

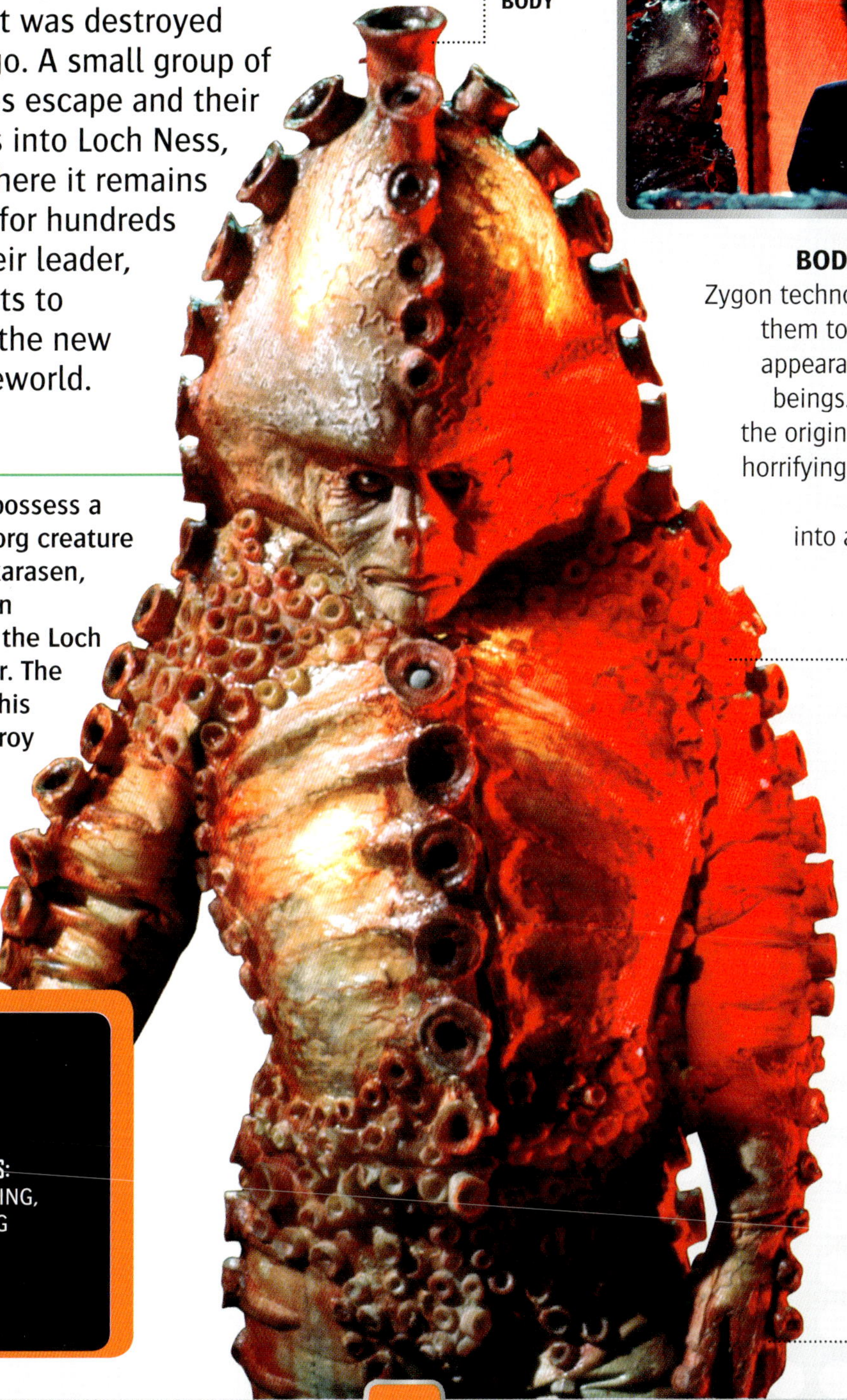

The Zygons possess a massive cyborg creature called the Skarasen, which is often mistaken for the Loch Ness Monster. The Zygons use this "pet" to destroy oil rigs off the coast of Scotland.

DATA FILE

HOMEWORLD:
UNNAMED

SPECIAL ABILITIES:
SHAPE-CHANGING, BODY COPYING

DOCTORS MET:
4TH

INDEX

Main entries are listed in **bold**

A

B

C

D

E

INDEX CONTINUED

T, U

V

W

X, Y, Z

LONDON, NEW YORK, MELBOURNE, MUNICH AND DELHI

Senior Editors: Victoria Taylor, Garima Sharma
Editors: Emma Grange, Kath Hill, Rahul Ganguly
Senior Designers: Clive Savage, Neha Ahuja
Designers: Mark Richards, Era Chawla, Suzena Sengupta
Jacket Designer: Mark Penfound
DTP Designer: Anurag Trivedi
Publishing Manager: Julie Ferris
Managing Editor: Laura Gilbert
Design Manager: Maxine Pedliham
Art Director: Ron Stobbart
Publisher: Simon Beecroft
Publishing Director: Alex Allan
Pre-Production Producer: Siu Chan
Senior Producer: Shabana Shakir

This edition published in 2013
First published in Great Britain in 2013 by

Dorling Kindersley Limited
80 Strand, London WC2R 0RL
Penguin Group (UK)

008-187858-Apr/2013

A CIP catalogue record for this book is available from the British Library.

ISBN: 978-1-4093-5090-3

Colour reproduction by Altaimage Ltd, UK
Printed and bound in China by South China Printing Company Ltd.

ACKNOWLEDGEMENTS

Dorling Kindersley would like to thank the following:

Annabel Gibson, Moray Laing and Jason Loborik; Jo Casey, Pamela Afram and Alan Cowsill for their editorial assistance; and Rhys Thomas and Lynne Moulding for design assistance.

From the BBC:
Executive Producers: Steven Moffat, Caroline Skinner
Drama Account Manager: Edward Russell
Brand Strategy Manager: Matt Nicholls
Script Editors: Richard Cookson, Derek Ritchie
Picture Campaign Manager: Alex Thompson
Creative Executives: Georgie Britton, Stephanie Milner
Brand Assets Co-ordinator: Bhirel Patel

Discover more at
www.dk.com
www.bbc.co.uk/doctorwho